I Didn't Know I Was Dead

Olivia Kristin

The story about what killed me and who saved me.

ms. Lisa,
you will live
not die!
♡

I DIDN'T KNOW I WAS DEAD

II

I DIDN'T KNOW I WAS DEAD

Ephesians 2:1-7

Once you were dead because of your disobedience and your many sins. You used to live in sin, just like the rest of the world, obeying the devil—the commander of the powers in the unseen world. He is the spirit at work in the hearts of those who refuse to obey God. All of us used to live that way, following the passionate desires and inclinations of our sinful nature. By our very nature we were subject to God's anger, just like everyone else. But God is so rich in mercy, and He loved us so much, that even though we were dead because of our sins, He gave us life when He raised Christ from the dead. (It is only by God's grace that you have been saved!) For He raised us from the dead along with Christ and seated us with Him in the heavenly realms because we are united with Christ Jesus. So God can point to us in all future ages as examples of the incredible wealth of His grace and kindness toward us, as shown in all He has done for us who are united with Christ Jesus.

I DIDN'T KNOW I WAS DEAD

I Didn't Know I was Dead
By Olivia Kristin

ISBN 9781091913479

Cover Design
Troy Howard | Skylynart | www.skylynart.com

Graphic Character Image— Dayona Rogiers

DEDICATION

This book is dedicated to...

My parents, grandparents, and great aunt

Morris & Kim Smith

Booker & Bonitta Smith

Sandra Leatherbury

Katie Smith

Jodella Doneghy

I thank God every day that He assigned me to you. I would not be who I am today nor would I have accomplished all I have if it wasn't for your example, support, and unconditional love. I honor you and I love you. Thank you for always seeing more in me than what I saw in myself!

To my mother, Kim—

Thank you for your obedience in naming me,

Olivia, *'Bringer of Peace'*

Kristin, *'Follower of Christ'*

In loving memory of,

Anita L. "Mammaw" Leatherbury

Michael E. "Pawpaw" Leatherbury

I DIDN'T KNOW I WAS DEAD

VI

CONTENTS

I DIDN'T KNOW I WAS DEAD

VIII

CHAPTER ONE

THE WAKE-UP CALL

There is a path before each person that seems right,
but it ends in death.
Proverbs 14:12

It was about one in the morning, and I was in my apartment.

I was sitting on my knees in my bathroom with tears running down my face.

The only words I could muster up the courage to say were, "Lord, I am sorry".

My whole life had changed and I had gotten myself into such a mess.

Sitting outside of my bathroom door was my boyfriend.

He was waiting for "closure" and a clear answer.

I knew I wanted to be done for good this time, but I felt stuck.

This was not our first go around.

We had broken up time and time again, yet I always ended up going back and wanting more.

He was my addiction...

The drug disguised as what I thought was love, that I couldn't get enough of.

Yet, this time, I wanted out!

I stood up, wiped my tears, and opened the door.

He was sitting on my vanity stool next to my television as I walked out of the bathroom. I walked passed him and as I sat down, he immediately restarted our conversation. This conversation was led by him and consisted of everything I did to ruin our relationship and everything I needed to work on. As the conversation continued, he began to move closer to me. With each word he took another step until he was right in my face.

Now hovering over me he asked, "You really want to break up with me"?

I DIDN'T KNOW I WAS DEAD

Yes, I replied.

He picked up my laptop and threw it across the room, grabbed me by my ankle and looked me right in my eyes for what seemed like forever.

All I could say was, "please don't".

Releasing his grip, he let go, walked down my steps, and left.

I quickly ran downstairs after I heard the door slam and locked the door. I had an alarm that I had never used the entire two years I lived in that apartment, but something told me to turn it on.

After turning it on, I ran back upstairs to wake up my roommate. I sat on her bed crying, informing her not only of what was happening that night, but an overview of the toxic relationship that she only knew in part. Now fully awake, she sat up in defense mode.

Then, the house alarm went off.

He's back.

I DIDN'T KNOW I WAS DEAD

"You gave him a key?"

No! I replied.

While realizing he must have made one, the alarm stopped.

Our alarm wasn't one that was connected to calling the police, it only made a noise when the door opened. Since the alarm stopped we knew the door was closed but we didn't know if he was inside or outside of the house. I was too afraid to move, so my roommate got up and went downstairs to see. She came back upstairs and said he wasn't there.

The alarm must have freighted him...

We sat and continued to talk until I realized I did not have my phone. He must have taken it, I told her. We tracked the phone on my laptop (which thank God was not broken) and saw that my phone was circling around our neighborhood.

He was still nearby.

I DIDN'T KNOW I WAS DEAD

I literally crawled across the floor to avoid him seeing my shadow.

I saw him pull into a parking spot, turn off his lights, sit, and then leave. I knew he kept my phone so that I would call him and give him an excuse to reenter, but I wanted no parts.

It was about four in the morning now, and my roommate wanted to lay down. I tried to sleep as well by lying next to her, but I couldn't.

While lying down, I heard a car speeding by and tires screeching.

I turned off all the lights in the house so he would think I was sleeping, and began crawling on the floor again to peak out the window.

He was circling around our apartment complex like a madman!

This went on for about thirty minutes...

Refusing to let my roommate call anyone or the police, I sat up that night completely awake in fear.

Hi— I appreciate you picking up this book! We started off pretty intense, I know, but I don't want you to put this book down. I believe there is no such thing as coincidences and that you have this book in your hand for a reason. I'm praying for you right now. I'm praying that your eyes will be open, that your heart will be softened, and that you will gain revelation to know if you are living or if you are a part of the walking dead, as I was. I pray your life begins to change for the better after picking up this book. I pray that God breathes on every area of your life in this very moment. I pray you begin to get vulnerable just as I am and will continue to be. I pray you look within your life to seek areas you need to change. Maybe you have had thoughts of no longer wanting to live? Maybe you have been feeling stuck or stagnant? Or maybe you are happy, but don't realize you're not living a life with purpose. Regardless of where you are in this current moment, I'm thankful you're here and I'm praying for you

Now let's get back to the story...

CHAPTER TWO

CHOICES

If it hurts you more than it helps you, it will eventually destroy you. You're strong enough to let go and brave enough to recover.

Sarah Jakes Roberts

My boyfriend and I had just started Whole 30 at the beginning of the year. If you aren't familiar with Whole 30, let me briefly explain. Whole 30 is a 30-day program where you strip certain foods from your diet completely such as sugar, grains, dairy, and legumes. The only foods you consume are grass fed meats, fruits, and vegetables. Most days while on this cleanse, I went without eating because I didn't adequately prepare.

It was not an intentional fast, but I gained clarity. I began to open up more about how I had been battling depression, although it took me time to accept that's what was going on. I felt like day after day, time was passing and I was just existing. I was having crying spells where I would burst into tears without providing a reason why. I had very little motivation to do what I once enjoyed, and I couldn't make it through that time in my life without smoking weed.

I was extremely needy and emotional! If I didn't have weed I was irritable and I would lash out at my boyfriend without an explainable reason. I remember throwing my water bottle at the back of his head while he was walking down the steps because of how upset I was.

I was not the Olivia I had once known...

Thank God, things began to happen during this time I didn't realize were for my good.

I was requested to take photos at The City of David on the south side of Columbus, Ohio. On the specific date they requested, I already had plans to attend a professional football game so I respectfully declined and referred someone else. Yet, they insisted that they wanted me to take the photos and picked a different weekend.

I wasn't regularly attending a church at the time but I was willing to break up my routine since they were paying me. I stayed for the entire service and took photos of praise and worship as well as the sermon.

When the service was coming to a close, Prophet Cornelius Hale asked if anyone wanted prayer. I hesitated but stood up because I knew I needed it. I stood at the altar as he laid his hands on my head and prayed in The Holy Spirit. Nothing dramatic happened and I didn't feel different right away. But little did I know, I just received a divine touch from God...

Looking at my phone as I got into my car after service, I saw the text message,

Church was never three hours... grab olive oil on your way back please. Trying to cook.

Hurrying home, I stopped and grabbed olive oil. I walked in the house to see my boyfriend preparing meals for us for the week. I gave him a big hug and kiss and then went upstairs to roll a blunt. I was extremely grateful for him! Like I mentioned before, I was battling depression and any help that would make my day easier, I needed!

That night we smoked, ate, laughed, watched TV, and talked all night. Then, the next morning, I went to work and my feelings spiraled down again. In one of my moods, I texted my boyfriend and told him I just wanted to be by myself after work.

Ok, Olivia. He responded.

9

I DIDN'T KNOW I WAS DEAD

While lying in my bed thinking I would be alone that night, suddenly, I heard my front door open.

It wasn't my roommate...

It was my boyfriend.

He came in the house, slammed the door behind him, walked upstairs to my room, and began to grab all of his stuff.

I ran out of the house, got in my car, and just began to drive.

Why you ask?

I couldn't tell you.

I was just serious about wanting to be alone.

I drove around for about thirty minutes with no destination in mind. I listened to music while looking at all of the beautiful homes in my area until deciding to head back to the house.

I DIDN'T KNOW I WAS DEAD

When I got back home, he was still there sitting in my room waiting for me...

We ended up fighting.

This fight ended with him throwing my phone into the wall leaving a a big whole, him leaving with some of my belongings, and sending a text saying,

Let me know about the wall somehow and I'll get somebody
to drop your stuff and money off.
Other than that, I'm blocking you just FYI.
Bags on porch.
Laptop under couch.

We did not speak at all the next day but I came home from work and saw a letter sitting on my bed as well as my stuff he had taken the night before. Naïve at the time (or just high), I did not even think about how he got in my house to leave everything on my bed...

I just laid down and went to sleep.

The letter was about two pages front and back. It was an overview of our relationship for the past couple of years, and ended with an apology about how he could not be the man I needed, and us not needing to be together.

I've done it again... I've made him upset... now it's over...

I texted him the next day saying,

I got your letter last night.
I never wanted things to be over between us...
all I asked for Monday was to be by myself.
I guess this may be best though.
But I forgive you and I love you.
Thank you for returning my things.

I got no response for three days.

What an addiction.

Manipulation and deception are two of the many ways the enemy distracts us from living a life of purpose. The enemy comes to steal, kill, and destroy. He comes to steal our purpose, kill our dreams, and destroy our life. I pray you are looking at the bigger picture and not just reading a story about myself and one of my ex-boyfriends. My ex-boyfriend, or whomever he sounds like in your life, is not the enemy. If that is your thought, let's correct it now and let's begin to recognize the spirits at work behind all of this.

I DIDN'T KNOW I WAS DEAD

I write this to you with reference to those who would deceive you [seduce and lead you astray].
1 John 2:26-28 AMPC

Deceitful, unclean spirits are always lurking in the shadows, looking for some way to dissuade us from faithfully following God. We need to be on our guard at all times. Their insinuations are deceptive, manipulative, seductive, and alluring. Demons lure people from a position of stability into instability in an attempt to capture them in their web of lies.
James W. Goll

Warnings Against False Teachers
Now the Holy Spirit tells us clearly that in the last times some will turn away from the true faith; they will follow deceptive spirits and teachings that come from demons. These people are hypocrites and liars, and their consciences are dead.
1 Timothy 4:1-2 NLT

This is not a book to expose people but to shed light on demonic spirits that attempt or are successful in coming into each and every one our lives!

Ephesians 6:12 says, in New Living Translation,

For we are not fighting against flesh-and-blood enemies, but against evil rulers and authorities of the unseen world, against mighty powers in this dark world, and against evil spirits in the heavenly places.

Staying in God's will and having a relationship with Jesus Christ is how we stay protected and covered! Making the continual choices to stay outside of the will of God is how I found myself in places The Lord never intended for me to be.

Surrendering my life to Christ is a **choice.**

Choosing not to copy the behaviors of this world is a **choice.**

Choosing to change the way I think is a **choice.**

Staying in the will of God is a **choice.**

I DIDN'T KNOW I WAS DEAD

Dictionary.com defines choice as an act of selecting or making a decision when faced with two or more possibilities.

We all have choices to make.

You may be reading this book and perceiving me as the victim of this story. But it was my choice to get in the relationship, it was my choice to stay in the relationship, and it was my choice to leave. I was not a victim. That relationship was what I wanted!

> *You always have a choice...*
> *even when you don't have control.*
> Steven Furtick

Maybe you've been feeling stuck as I described...

Feeling stuck is dangerous!
We don't go anywhere because we believe we can't.

This is a belief, a very unhealthy one, that is a LIE, rooted in fear.

Believing we do not have a choice in situations is how we play the victim.

The definition of a victim from dictionary.com is a person who is harmed, injured, or killed as a result of a crime, accident, or other event or action. Another definition of victim is one who is tricked or duped. (Duped meaning deceived). I am not saying that some people are not victimized and need justice because there are many! On the other hand, there are some of us crying to be set free yet denying our free will to make the choice to break out of the things that are keeping us bound. Or, we refuse to be obedient and listen to wisdom, consequently allowing ourselves to be so easily subject to deception and manipulation.

Solomon wrote in Proverbs 1:30-33,

*They rejected my advice and paid no attention when I corrected them. Therefore, they must eat the bitter fruit of living their own way, choking on their own schemes. For simpletons turn away from me—**to death**. Fools destroyed by their own complacency. But all who listen to me will live in peace, untroubled by fear of harm.*

We are all given choices in life.

Some choices I knew were good and others in my conscience I knew were not good for me.
But I made them anyway...

All it takes is one unwise choice to change our lives forever.

If I hadn't made the choice to leave the relationship I was in and to surrender my life to Christ, I would not have written this book. My obedience to leave was not only about me and my life, but it was about you too!

Whose freedom is on hold due to your choice to live or not to live right?

My example so far has been a past relationship but for you it may be something else that is deceiving you. It may be obvious to others such as: drugs, alcohol, your unhealthy eating habits, gambling, a relationship: whether intimate, personal or corporate, or even the bitterness you're holding onto from unhealed wounds. Or, it can be something or someone that's not easily recognizable. Whatever or whomever it is, I pray The Lord speaks to you clearly to not only discover what or who it is, but to start making the right choices to break free from it. I pray that The Lord gives you the spirit of discernment to be able to see past titles, position, money, and power.

Not everything or everyone that looks and sounds good is God.

17

There Is Only One Good News

*I am shocked that you are turning away so soon from God,
who called you to himself through the loving mercy of
Christ. You are following a different way that pretends to be
the Good News but is not the Good News at all. You are
being fooled by those who deliberately twist the truth
concerning Christ. Let God's curse fall on anyone, including
us or even an angel from heaven, who preaches a different
kind of Good News than the one we preached to you. I say
again what we have said before: If anyone preaches any
other Good News than the one you welcomed, let that
person be cursed.*
Galatians 1:6-9 NLT

A week or so passed after our last fight and my boyfriend
and I began talking again. Then he started coming over
again. Another episode of the toxic abuse cycle continued.
He came over on the Sunday before my "wake-up call". We
talked all night and smoked as usual. Then, he told me he
didn't want to be with me anymore. He said things were way
too confusing. After telling me this, he went downstairs to
sleep on my couch. Since he was now a floor away, I
continued our conversation by laying in my bed and texting
him.

18

I DIDN'T KNOW I WAS DEAD

Throwing myself a pity party, I told him I think he should just leave me alone for good. I told him I needed to move away, do some soul searching, get over him, and move on. I was being manipulative because I did not want him to leave, but knew I would get a reaction out of him by saying, *just leave me alone for good... I need to move away.*

You manipulate me, I manipulate you.
I manipulate you, you manipulate me.

Toxic cycle!

I ended up calling off work the next morning because I just couldn't drag myself out of bed. It was one of those long nights you wake up with your eyes swollen shut. So instead of going to work, I laid in bed all day.

Our conversations were really brief this entire week until that Thursday.

Then, Thursday came...
I received his text message asking if he could come over to my place and watch Scandal. We loved Scandal! We weren't on good terms by any means, but what else was new. So, I

made the choice to let him come over. When he came over we did not watch Scandal at all, but instead I was bombarded by insults and confusing topics of conversations. This was the night I spoke of in chapter one, so you know how it ended...

The next morning after my "wake-up call" I attempted to get my phone back. I called him, his friends, and where he worked, looking like the crazy woman I had turned into trying to explain what happened, but no one believed me. I was pitiful! He told everyone he did not have my phone and I must have misplaced it. All day Friday I was without it, tearing up my house searching for it where he said he left it, and then later even popped up at his job looking for it.

At this point I was looking super crazy!

Finally, I went back home and gave up.

Saturday came, and I got a message from him on Facebook saying my phone was in my apartment's leasing office. I went to the leasing office and there it was. I turned the phone back on but had to wait thirty minutes after too many unsuccessful password attempts. While waiting to be able to

use it, I pulled myself together because I had two
photoshoot appointments. I went through the motions to do
what I had to do, but I was far from being present.

Sunday came and I attempted to watch church on live
stream, but couldn't focus. All I could think about was how I
got myself so deep into this situation?

> *You were dead before you checked in.*
> *You've been drifting.*
> *Nobody wakes up addicted.*
> *Every great fall is from a hundred bad decisions.*
> KB— Art of Drifting

I laid in bed all day scrolling through social media, mad at
myself and the world for being so stupid.

That night I called my grandmother with tears running down
my face and a shaky voice and said, *I need to tell you
something...*

I DIDN'T KNOW I WAS DEAD

The Lord is close to the brokenhearted; he rescues those whose spirits are crushed.

Psalms 34:18

CHAPTER THREE

RESUSCITATION

Code Blue. 6ᵗʰ Floor Room 612.
Code Blue. 6ᵗʰ Floor Room 612.

When we hear this on the loud speaker, everyone in the area knows to begin running to the announced room. This includes grabbing the crash cart, delegating tasks, and someone initiating chest compressions right away!

MediceneNet defines Code Blue as: An emergency situation announced in a hospital or institution in which a patient is in cardiopulmonary arrest, requiring a team of providers (sometimes called a 'code team') to rush to the specific location and begin immediate resuscitative efforts.

Those in the medical field and even those who are not in the medical field, know that when someone is in a code blue situation, time can determine life or death.

I'm thankful that when I was going through one of the most difficult times of my life I had my grandmother, Sandra Leatherbury, to intercede for me on my behalf. The day I went over her house and told her everything that happened,

23

she did not leave me alone. I rededicated my life to Jesus Christ and received the baptism of The Holy Spirit. From that day forward, she called me daily, she prayed for me, allowed me to stay with her, and she asked important questions to make sure I wasn't getting off track.

If you're going through a tragedy and need help, please seek it! The choices you make during this time are pivotal to your future self. If you're not going through a life defining moment but know someone who is- run towards them (with wisdom) Code Blue! They not only need your intercession but divine intervention!

Until the alarm sounds, all throughout the hospital and everyone can hear that someone is in cardiac arrest, no one knows that person is in their room dying without any help. Or, in a non-hospital situation, if you see someone who is not breathing and/or without a pulse you know to begin CPR.

In a code blue situation, we are talking about someone who is about to die a physical death but what about those of us who are dead spiritually, mentally, and/or emotionally? Why are we not in the same quick pursuit to come alive again or quick to help those around us come alive again?

Or, is it because we just aren't aware... that we are dying...?

Just as we need to know if someone needs **CPR** by assessing them:

Are they breathing?

Do they have a pulse?

We need to look for signs within ourselves and within our loved ones to know if we are dying and/or dead!

I'll go a little deeper as I explain what I mean by being dead emotionally, mentally, and spiritually.

Emotionally Dead

People who are emotionally healthy are able to have control over their thoughts, feelings, and their behaviors. Emotionally healthy people are able to cope with life's challenges and can bounce back when they have setbacks. People who are emotionally healthy feel good about themselves as well as others, resulting in them being able to have good relationships. Someone who is emotionally dead or emotionally unhealthy will have the opposite symptoms.

Being emotionally healthy does not mean you're happy all of the time, instead means that you are aware of your emotions and are able to regulate them.

I took an emotional intelligence course in 2018. One of the teachers whom is also my mentor Mrs. Lynette Vaive says, "No feelings are bad. Rather, it's how we handle our feelings".

For instance, anger is not a "bad" emotion. We will be angry and some things should make us angry! But, we cannot go busting through someone's window or lighting buildings on fire just because we are upset. We have to be able to control that anger.

The bible says in Ephesians 4:26, New Kings James Version, *"Be angry, and do not sin": do not let the sun go down on your wrath".*

We cannot let our emotions control us!

Be angry?
Yes!
Sin?
No!

We have the choice to have control over our emotions and we must choose to make wise choices regardless of how we feel.

I DIDN'T KNOW I WAS DEAD

Are you in control of your emotions?
Or do they have control over you?

Holding onto bitterness and anger toward a person is a sign of being emotionally unhealthy. We will talk about this more in a later chapter that unforgiveness causes sickness! I don't know about you, but I am not trying to die from being bitter. It is important that we learn to let things go. It is not easy, but it is a choice. A choice to be open and willing.

Are you holding a grudge against someone?

Not being thankful causes us to be emotionally unhealthy. I have woken up too many times not looking forward to going to my job or being around certain people and my head was filled with negative thoughts. Next thing I knew, I was going to bed with a depressed spirit because I allowed my negative thinking to drag me down all day. I was full of complaints, instead of being full of thanksgiving.

Thank you, God, for a job that provides me with money for myself and/or my family!
Thank you, God, for my health!
Thank you, God, for a life to live!

I DIDN'T KNOW I WAS DEAD

Try it and make it a habit to be thankful!

Instead, they grumbled in their tents
and refused to obey the Lord.
Psalm 106:25 NLT

Do everything without complaining and arguing.
Philippians 2:14 NLT

Ignoring our feelings causes us to be emotionally unhealthy.
I definitely was one who attempted to ignore my feelings. I
knew I was depressed and I knew I was unhappy so I
enjoyed smoking weed. I wanted to be high because I didn't
want to feel the lows. I remember listening to an old Drake
song in high school. He said, "I be getting high to balance
out the lows". The song is actually called Fear. How ironic
right? We fear feeling pain. When it's during painful
moments we learn something. A very good friend of mine,
Paris Miles, told me one day as she was doing my hair, "we
are supposed to feel the highs and the lows in life". She's
right. This is one reason why I personally stopped smoking
weed, and I loved to smoke weed! I loved how it made me
feel, I loved how it made food taste better, and I loved how
much stronger my laughs were. What I didn't like, though,

was not being able to discern the voice of God. I also di
like that I did not have control over my emotions becau:
the weed had control over me. I was dependent on it!

Lastly, denying the impact of our past on our present
causes us to be emotionally unhealthy. A lot of us attempt to
ignore what may have happened in our childhood, our
teenage years, young adult years, or even our adult life that
still has a significant impact on us. We are told we need to
move on, but instead of being healed from situations we only
bury the feelings. It's like covering a gunshot wound with a
Band-Aid when the wound needs to be open to heal. We
cannot hide our brokenness or our failures and believe that
we will just "be okay". No, we need healing!

Pray

Lord, help me to have full control over my emotions. You
gave me emotions to be able to feel, to live, and to hear from
you. Things in life will hurt me Lord. Things in life have
hurt me. Things in my life will bring me joy. Thank You for
everything that has brought me joy. Help me Lord to be
content in all situations and all seasons. Help me to continue
to mature so that I may be effective in whatever season I'm
in. I thank you Lord right now for giving me a soft heart, to
feel the way you do, but also the strength to not be easily

offended, a worry bug, or bitter by refusing to let things go. Heal me Lord and make me whole. In Jesus Name, Amen.

He said to her, "Daughter, your faith has healed you. Go in peace and be freed from your suffering."

Mark 5:34 NIV

Mentally Dead

MentalHealth.gov describes Mental Health as our emotional, psychological, and social well-being. It affects how we think, feel, and act. It also helps determine how we handle stress, relate to others, and make choices. Mental health is important at every stage of life, from childhood and adolescence through adulthood. It further explains that mental health has many contributing factors such as biological factors, genes, brain chemistry, life experiences, such as trauma or abuse, or a family history of mental health problems.

Early warning signs of mental health problems include:

- eating or sleeping too much or too little
- pulling away from people and usual activities
- having low or no energy

- feeling numb or like nothing matters
- having unexplained aches and pains
- feeling helpless or hopeless
- smoking, drinking, or using drugs more than usual
- feeling unusually confused, forgetful, on edge, angry, upset, worried, or scared
- yelling or fighting with family and friends
- experiencing severe mood swings that cause problems in relationships
- having persistent thoughts and memories you can't get out of your head
- hearing voices or believing things that are not true
- inability to perform daily tasks like taking care of your kids or getting to work or school
- depression
- feelings of extreme highs and lows
- excessive fears
- social withdrawal
- inability to cope with daily problems
- thinking of harming yourself or others

In addition, confusion is a sign of being mentally unhealthy. Confusion is defined as a lack of understanding or uncertainty. A situation of panic; a breakdown of order, a disorderly jumble.

1 Corinthians 14:33 says,

For God is not the author of confusion but of peace.

The enemy does not want us to have peace of mind. He wants to confuse us into thinking that we do not belong or that something is wrong with us. He wants us to be so disrupted in our minds that we no longer want to live.

If you're currently battling depression and/or thinking about committing suicide please seek help from a mental health professional or trusted adult. The national suicide prevention lifeline is 1-800-273-8255 (TALK) and/or you can text the crisis text line 4HOPE.

Please pray this prayer with me—
Dear Lord, thank you for making me and putting me on this earth with purpose. Thank you for loving me, for choosing me as your very own, and for ordering my steps. I am not feeling well, Lord. I have had thoughts of no longer wanting

to live and I've been hopeless. Help me God! Jesus come into my life. Help me to find hope again. Help me to find joy again. Help me to love again. Help me to have peace of mind and peace in my heart. Lord, I do not want to die, I want to live! I know, Lord, that I have purpose and I am here on this earth to make a difference. I am talented, I am loved, and no one can do what you have called me to do like I can. (I will live, I will not die) Thank you, Jesus, for coming into my life, for helping me on this journey, and for being a light to lead me out of this darkness I'm feeling. I thank you Lord for healing me right now at this very moment. For healing my mind, my body, and my soul. In Jesus Name, Amen.

Olivia's tag line

I pray you are not ashamed to admit the feelings you feel as I once was. I also pray you are not ashamed to see a licensed therapist or medical doctor.

Spiritually Dead

Does it strike you, as it has me, that there is something terribly wrong with a passionless, passive, mundane, monotonous relationship with God? Aren't we vaguely unsettled with the idea that somehow a daily relationship with God... the God of the universe... can end up with the flavor of stale bread? The Bible is clear that our passion and spiritual fervor should be constant. (Romans 12:11) So why have so many Christians accepted a faith experience that is

*so far below what God intended for them? A passionate,
thriving relationship with God should be the norm, not the
exception, for every follower of Christ.*
Stovall Weems
(Awakening: A New Approach to Faith, Fasting, and
Spiritual Freedom)

Romans 12:11-12 says,

*Never be lazy but work hard and serve the Lord
enthusiastically. Rejoice in our confident hope. Be patient in
trouble and keep on praying.*

Signs/Symptoms you have become spiritually dead:
- you treat faith like a routine not a ritual
  - routine— life of check marking the boxes of minimal obedience and compliance.
  - ritual— there's meaning, value, purpose, mission, and passion in what you do because of Jesus.
- you lack passion
- you treat church like you have to go not you get to go
- you've closed your eyes to Jesus's mission
- hardened heart
  - disobedient—no longer feel convictions

- you care about platforms more than loving God's people
- you care more about recognition than sharing The Gospel
- you stop believing in what God can and will do

The Lord says:

These people come near to me with their mouth
and honor me with their lips,
but their hearts are far from me.
Their worship of me is based on merely human rules they
have been taught.

Isaiah 29:13 NIV

I love to reflect on when I first came back home to Christ and how excited I was to talk about Jesus. I was just like the woman at the well. (Read John 4:1-42)

I remember how excited I was to go home and read my bible, to pray, to dance, to worship, to journal, and to tell others about how God delivered me. I also remember myself in different seasons, when God didn't seem as close anymore. Seasons where everything was going wrong, people were turning on me, my debt kept getting thicker and thicker, and I felt as though I was getting punished. Can I be honest? I wasn't as excited to go to church. I wasn't as excited to raise my hands during praise and worship and I wasn't as excited to volunteer as I would've been if everything was going well. I'm a spoiled brat! When I'm not getting my way, I resort to pouting mode. I had to learn that God loves me, but is not bothered by my temper tantrums. That was a tough lesson for me to swallow.

Our temper tantrums only distract us in seeing what God wants us to see and do!

Our temper tantrums open the door to the enemy when they turn into an offense.

That offense can turn into disobedience, us falling away from God.

Our continual disobedience can cause our hearts to be hardened to where we no longer feel the conviction of God.

Our hardened hearts can have us so far off the path God wants us to take, we ultimately end up lost and spiritually dead.

Then when we become spiritually dead, but are still in positions of influence, we begin to lead others the wrong way as well...

We can continue going to church, continue to clap our hands, stand and sit when the preacher instructs, volunteer and serve, yet be so detached from God Himself. Speaking and preaching Jesus, yet not bearing fruit or showing any characteristics of Christ.

Help us Lord!

We must be careful not to draw away and become lukewarm...

The bible is clear in Revelation 3:16,

So because you are lukewarm (spiritually useless), and neither hot nor cold, I will vomit you out of My mouth [rejecting you with disgust].

There are people always looking up to us. Dictionary.com defines looking as directing one's gaze toward and to think of or regard in a specified way. If we are representing Christ, how do people who do not know Christ regard Him by watching us?

Do you know there are people who don't believe in Jesus just by watching us? God is not the author of confusion. Who are you confusing by professing Christ yet living a lifestyle of darkness? How can we get this next generation who is unchurched to believe in Christ if we are living just as the world does?

The generation behind us, our children, grandchildren, nieces, nephews, peers, family, whomever we have influence over, is looking at us more than they are listening to us. It doesn't matter if we preach Jesus, have a Christian blog, scripture in our bio, go to church every Wednesday, Saturday, and Sunday, or have minster in front of our name. Are you showing them Jesus? The Lord is not pleased with those who honor Him with their mouths, yet their lifestyles do not match. If you have two different lifestyles, a public life and a private life, it doesn't matter who you believe you are hiding from, you can't hide from God. Make it straight, and repent. If you do not listen to The Lord's correction when He attempts to correct you in private, He will begin to expose your private life, publicly.

For there is nothing hidden that will not be revealed, and nothing concealed that will not be brought to light.

Mark 4:22

Whose life are you leading down the wrong path due to your disobedience?

But if you cause one of these little ones who trusts in me to fall into sin, it would be better for you to have a large millstone tied around your neck and be drowned in the depths of the sea. What sorrow awaits the world, because it tempts people to sin. Temptations are inevitable, but what sorrow awaits the person who does the tempting.

Matthew 18:6-7

Pray

Father God, breathe life on me again. Forgive me Lord for entering into a routine and treating a relationship with you as one that is not desirable. Forgive me for being disobedient to your Holy Spirit. Forgive me for living a lukewarm lifestyle. I repent, Lord. Come into my life and rule my life. Soften my heart Lord God and allow me to hear your voice over any other. Help me to live for you, being set apart for all that you have for me. Help me to continue to mature, being joyful and obedient in all seasons. Give me your strength to continue to push forward regardless of my circumstances. As I draw near to you, draw near to me Lord. Thank you for never leaving me or forsaking me even when I don't deserve your presence. Thank you for being such an amazing Heavenly Father. In Jesus Name, Amen.

If the Lord convicted you on somethings that are not pleasing to Him please don't ignore it. The world needs you spiritually healthy. Let go of the double lifestyles.

Asking for help is not a sign of weakness! After reading about the characteristics of being dead emotionally, spiritually, and or mentally, do any apply to you?

Regardless if you're feeling alive and well or if you are slowly dying, I want you to get an accountability partner. Someone you can trust to tell the truth, and who will not judge you, but love you and be able to help you.

I DIDN'T KNOW I WAS DEAD

If one person falls, the other can reach out and help. But someone who falls alone is in real trouble.

Ecclesiastes 4:10 NLT

If you know someone that has fallen away from the truth, please pray for them and do not judge them. But remember, we all need forgiveness, grace, and mercy.

Live creatively, friends. If someone falls into sin, forgivingly restore him, saving your critical comments for yourself. You might be needing forgiveness before the day's out. Stoop down and reach out to those who are oppressed. Share their burdens, and so complete Christ's law. If you think you are too good for that, you are badly deceived.

Galatians 6:1-3 MSG

If you have fallen away from The Truth, don't be ashamed! I thank God you're here!

You were running [the race] well; who has interfered and prevented you from obeying the truth?
Galatians 5:7 AMP

41

<u>Pray</u>

Thank you, Lord, for giving me the revelation that in certain areas of my life I am dying and/or already dead emotionally, mentally, and/or spiritually. Thank you, Lord, for your grace, kindness, mercy, and patience with me. Thank you, Lord, that I do not need to stay dead because you've died on the cross for me. Thank you, Father God, for waking me up so that I can live and live life abundantly! I declare that I will live and I will not die and declare the works of the Lord. Live big in me Jesus! My life will never be the same. In Jesus Name, Amen.

CHAPTER FOUR

WHEN DID I DIE?

The serpent was the shrewdest of all the wild animals the Lord God had made. One day he asked the woman, "Did God really say you must not eat the fruit from any of the trees in the garden?" "Of course we may eat fruit from the trees in the garden," the woman replied. "It's only the fruit from the tree in the middle of the garden that we are not allowed to eat. God said, 'you must not eat it or even touch it; if you do, you will die.'" "You won't die!" the serpent replied to the woman. "God knows that your eyes will be opened as soon as you eat it, and you will be like God, knowing both good and evil." The woman was convinced. She saw that the tree was beautiful and its fruit looked delicious, and she wanted the wisdom it would give her. So she took some of the fruit and ate it. Then she gave some to her husband, who was with her, and he ate it, too. At that moment their eyes were opened, and they suddenly felt shame at their nakedness. So they sewed fig leaves together to cover themselves.

Genesis 3:1-7 NLT

Back in the eighth grade you would've never heard a cuss word come out of my mouth. That just wasn't who I was. I went to church and I was known as the good girl at my school. Some of my friends and classmates had boyfriends, wore thongs, which I thought was so disgusting in middle school, made out with their boyfriends before practice, smoked and sold black and milds, and drank alcohol. I, on the other hand, wanted no parts at the time. Until I realized I began to attract boys. Not only because of my appearance, but because of my mature body for a teenager. Not to mention, I could dance. I liked the attention I began to get. Majority of my classmates were having sex. So, although I knew from listening in church I should wait until I was married, I wanted to see what the hype was about.

I dated a guy my freshman year in high school. It was the most innocent and pure relationship ever. Neither one of us drove so if we went out together our parents would take us. We mostly just spoke on the phone though because we did not go to the same school. He would text me every night even when I was being the spoiled brat I am, "I love you, have a good night's rest". (I thought that was the most annoying thing ever). I couldn't understand why he was so nice, there was no excitement in that. After a year of dating, we broke up, because there was a rumor he cheated on me. I didn't believe it was true but I thought what a good reason to get out. So, I was done.

The next guy I dated was more exciting in my eyes. I loved the attention he showed me publicly and the way he made me feel. He told me he loved me too. In this relationship I lost my virginity. I remember sitting in my room multiple times thinking about making the decision to have sex. My boyfriend and I spoke about it but he told me he would wait until I was ready and knew for sure I wanted to do it. He already had sex before so I remembered thinking that if I didn't have sex with him, he wouldn't stay with me. I wanted to make sure he loved me more than any other girls he dated so I decided to make that big girl decision.

Losing my virginity was not the only thing I experienced in this relationship. It was also the first intimate relationship that included mental and verbal abuse. I got cheated on, manipulated, and embarrassed in front of my peers publicly and on social media. Because we were sexually active and he was my first I was extremely blinded by how I was being treated. I also frequently got in trouble from my parents for being disobedient and lying when it came to where I was and what I was doing. We dated on and off for years in high school and college. It was a relationship I did not heal from that consequently put me in a cycle where I continued to make the wrong choices, not only in relationships, but for myself. I wanted to prove myself after this relationship. I wanted to show everyone who Olivia was, even though I hadn't realized I lost her. I wanted to be accepted, liked, and loved so bad, not by God but by people. I've always desired marriage and have always been a sucker for a good love story, but instead of following God's will for my life I attempted to find love my own way. At the time I had not known how not healing from my first intimate relationship would affect the next ten years of my life...

I was so easily deceived, manipulated, and consequently was abused in multiple relationships because of a lack of knowing my purpose.

> *Where purpose is not known, abuse is inevitable.*
> Dr. Myles Munroe

So, when did I die? Somewhere between transitioning from a child to a teenager. As a child I vividly remember how much fun I had being alone. I have a huge age gap between myself and my siblings so I played a lot by myself. I remember making up games, going outside and exploring because I thought I was Harriet The Spy, and making up dances to later teach to my friends. I loved church, being around my family, dancing, and writing books and poetry. I loved all of these things not because anyone else loved them, but because these things brought me joy!

Erik Erikson developed a model regarding human development throughout our lifespan that includes eight psychosocial stages. Each stage is associated with a conflict or crisis that arises during a developmental period in our life, that we must successfully resolve in order to proceed in our development. Erik Erikson's Theory of Psychological Development describes ages 13-21 as Identity vs. Role Confusion. Erikson believed the major task of the adolescence is forming their identity.

In an article, *Understanding Erikson's Theory of Psychological Development*, Kendra Cherry wrote,

One of the main elements of Erikson's psychosocial stage theory is the development of ego identity. It is the conscious self that we develop through social interaction, which is constantly changing due to new experiences and information we acquire in our daily interaction with others. During the identity verses role confusion stage, this conflict is centered on developing a personal identity. Successfully completing this stage leads to a strong sense of self that will remain throughout life.

In our adolescence years is when we are trying to find out who we are. During this pivotal time when I should have been asking God, who am I? What is Your purpose for my life? What are your plans for me? Instead, I was seeking validation from my peers, my accomplishments, and social media.

Identity vs. Role confusion

Instead of forming my identity I was confused about my role in life.

Successfully completing this stage leads to a strong sense of self that will remain throughout life.

I had not completed this stage, successfully I should say, until I came back home to Christ! I had not known my identity and whom I was so I was confused! If we do not know who we are in Christ we will continue to search and search and search for ourselves in everything and/or everyone! We spoke about this in the previous chapter, how confusion is mentally unhealthy. God is not the author of confusion!

"You won't die!" the serpent replied to the woman. "God knows that your eyes will be opened as soon as you eat it, and you will be like God, knowing both good and evil."

I compare Eve in The Garden of Eden talking to Satan to my life as a teenager making the choice to give my body away. I had known the consequences of sex before marriage

48

but nonetheless, I was curious. I wanted to know for myself what everyone else was talking about.

Curiosity is a strong desire to know or learn something. Satan knew Eve would be curious to know both good and evil which is how he manipulated her into eating the fruit God commanded her not to eat. The enemy knew I would compare myself to those around me and I, all too well, wanted to fit in. He knew I had a call on my life from the day I was born and wanted to stop it! He knew during this stage of finding my identity he had to intercede.

He may have interceded in your life as well at a young age and it is still affecting you now, but there's good news. God can turn your life around! I'm so thankful God causes all things to work together for the good of those who love God and are called according to His purpose. (Romans 8:28) Every unwise choice I made I share unashamed to stop someone else from making the same unwise decisions. We often don't realize how one choice has consequences that will last for years and years and years.

Just as God has a plan for our lives, so does Satan! Know God's plan, but also know Satan's and fight against it by staying in God's will and knowing His word.

I DIDN'T KNOW I WAS DEAD

Be sober, be vigilant; because your adversary the devil walks about like a roaring lion, seeking whom he may devour.

1 Peter 5:8

I didn't know that I had died the moment I no longer sought my identity from Christ.

I didn't know my desire to please people, instead of God, would have me entangled in years of abuse; not only from others but from myself.

The enemy is waiting to come after our teenagers during this time when they are trying to find themselves.

It is the conscious self that we develop through social interaction, which is constantly changing due to new experiences and information we acquire in our daily interaction with others.

There's so much information that our preteens and teens are receiving nowadays. So many conflicting voices from The Truth whether it's through social media, television, music, or at school. If we are not aware of what they are being exposed to, we will not be prepared to fight against the lies that are entering into their minds.

I DIDN'T KNOW I WAS DEAD

If we are not aware of what we are being exposed to, we will not be prepared to fight against the lies that are entering our minds either.

We must not neglect the curious questions of a teenager!

We must not rebuke them for asking questions!

We have to be transparent, tell them the truth, and our stories!

I've learned that every time I'm transparent, I stomp on the enemy's plan to put fear or shame into my heart and keep me silent.

I will write, I will speak, and I will prophesy!

Transparency with a purpose can be transformational.
Sam Chand

Everyone knows that I was the good girl. I did my best to make everyone happy with me. But then I found out that it was impossible to please the whole crowd, so I spoke up. & I spoke out. I learned that love doesn't hold its tongue and passion doesn't bow to what they think. It's you and me. Sometimes it's painful to be brave. To look fear in the face and know your name. To find your strength.
Steffany Gretzinger 'I Spoke Up'

If you are a preteen, teenager, or emerging adult pray this...
Dear God, thank you for making me in your image. Thank you for loving me and for giving me an identity. I know my identity is found in You. Lord, please protect me. Protect me physically, mentally, and spiritually. Help me to stay set apart Lord. Help me to be a good example to my friends and my family. Your word says, in 1 Timothy 4:12, Don't let anyone look down on me because I am young, but I will set an example for believers in my speech, in conduct, in love, in faith and in purity. Help me to stay pure Lord. Give me discernment, wisdom, and understanding. Show me my purpose God and give me Godly friendships and Godly mentors who will be good examples for me. Help me to be successful in my schoolwork and/or my work life and I pray that favor surrounds me all the days of my life. In Jesus Name, Amen.

If you have a preteen, teenager, or emerging adult that is your child, grandchild, sibling, niece, nephew, or you just love them pray this...
Father God, I thank you and I praise you for (insert their name and/or names). Thank you for allowing me to be an example in their life. Thank you, Lord, for our relationship. Father God, help me to be transparent and honest when

they ask me questions. I give my burdens to you Lord so that I am not taking my stress out on them. Help me, Lord, to do what I need to do so that they can be a child and not worry about what adults need to worry about. Protect them and watch over them. Keep them free from any hurt, harm, or danger. Cover them and give them Godly friendships. Give me discernment to know when certain relationships are not for them and give them ears to hear wisdom and Your voice through me. Show me what's not like You in me so that I can be the example I need to be. I release any feelings of guilt or shame that I have not done enough, for them. I thank You that today is a fresh start to teach, to love, and to guide them. In Jesus Name, Amen.

As a young adult and after coming back home to Christ I have been so overjoyed to find my love for all of the things I once loved as a child. The Lord gave me my desire to write, to create, and to dance again!

He wants to do the same for you!

Trust in the Lord and do good.

Then you will live safely in the land and prosper.

Take delight in the Lord,

and he will give you your heart's desires.

Commit everything you do to the Lord.

Trust him, and he will help you.

He will make your innocence radiate like the dawn,

and the justice of your cause will shine like the noonday

sun.

Psalm 37:3-6 NLT

CHAPTER FIVE

NEW LIFE/DYING AGAIN

Death works in us that life might work in others.

James W. Goll The Lifestyle of a Prophet

This means that anyone who belongs to Christ has become a new person. The old life is gone; a new life has begun!

2 Corinthians 5:17 NLT

So, I realize I am dead, come back Home to Christ, began living, all to die again?

What?

After rededicating my life to Christ, I knew I needed to make some necessary lifestyle changes in order to stay on track and not get distracted.

First lifestyle change— prayer and spending time in God's word.

I began to be intentional about my time in prayer and in God's word when I came back home to Christ. I knew that if I wanted to walk in God's will for my life I needed to know His will. How do we know His will? By communicating with

Him (Prayer) and by learning more about Him (The Bible). These two things are an absolute necessity in living a life for Christ. Replacing my extracurricular activities that did not give me life (gossiping, smoking, getting drunk, having sex outside of marriage) needed to be replaced with prayer and reading God's word.

Doesn't sound too appealing huh? Lol. That was my mindset as well, until I had the revelation that all of the things I chose to do outside of God's will were killing me.

Don't copy the behavior and customs of this world, but let God transform you into a new person by changing the way you think. Then you will learn to know God's will for you, which is good and pleasing and perfect.
Romans 12:2 NLT

Another lifestyle change I made was to stop smoking weed.

Weed for me was my escape from life. It was an easy and quick fix to stop feeling those feelings I wanted to avoid. Making the decision to stop avoiding those feelings gave The Lord room to show me the roots to where I needed to heal and heal me for good. Just because I chose to stop smoking weed didn't mean the people I was around were going to jump on that bandwagon too. I had to make the obedient and consistent decision to choose to stay sober regardless of the aroma coming into my room or wherever I chose to go where it was present.

> **Be sober** *[well balanced and self-disciplined], be alert and cautious at all times. That enemy of yours, the devil, prowls around like a roaring lion [fiercely hungry], seeking someone to devour.*
>
> 1 Peter 5:8 AMP

Another lifestyle change— stop having sex outside of marriage.

I was playing house with my boyfriend so fornicating was a consistent thing. Coming back home to Christ meant making the decision to give my body solely to Christ, saving myself until marriage. Was this easy? No. Sex is everywhere. Everywhere! Continuing to make this choice means choosing not to watch or listen to certain things anymore. I loved the show Power. But let's be real. It's a porno allowed on television! If you're making the decision to no longer partake in particular activities it is wise to resist certain temptations.

For this is the will of God, that you be sanctified [separated and set apart from sin]: that you abstain and back away from sexual immorality;

1 Thessalonians 4:3 AMP

Another lifestyle choice I made that I didn't see coming was denouncing from the Greek Organization, Alpha Kappa Alpha Sorority Incorporated.

I remember having lunch with my friend, Taylor Dunlap. It was one of the first times we connected intentionally and spoke together. She began to tell me about her experience with denouncing her Greek letters. She pledged AKA as well. She told me her testimony and how The Lord told her, "I called you to make disciples, not AKA's".

I thought that's nice sis, but The Lord told you that, not me. Period. I continued to do what The Lord was calling me to do in that season. I knew so many pastors who were AKA's as well and thought, well they do both, so I'm good!

The next couple of months after we met, I got a call from my little cousin. She called me to tell me she was interested in pledging a Greek organization and she wanted my advice. Honestly, I had the most generic and non-authentic answer

58

to her questions. I said, "It will take up a lot of your time, make sure it's something you truly want to do". Then, we got off the phone and I felt a major conviction. I wanted to say nooo, don't do it! I know you are searching for something and you are trying to figure out who you are, but it's not there! Yet, I was a part of a Greek organization myself. How hypocritical of me, so I said nothing.

Then I began hearing, "You were called to make disciples not AKA's".

Thanks Taylor....

People look up to us in regards to who we are and what we represent. I wasn't just an advocate for Christ, I was an advocate for Greek life.

I heard, you were called to make disciples not AKA's, over and over for the next couple of days. This was during a time when I was moving and packing up all of my belongings. When I went to take my diploma, business license, and AKA certificate off the wall, the glass broke on my AKA frame.

Okay God.

I have to let this go, too? What will people think? It's not that big of deal Lord, AKA is not an idol to me! I can hold onto it and still do what You are asking me to do!

Then, during my study time I came across the verse 1 John 5:21...

> *Dear children, keep away from anything that might take God's place in your hearts.*

Wow!

It didn't say that **DID** take God's place in your heart, it said that **MIGHT**.

Tim Keller said, *if anything becomes more fundamental than God to your happiness, meaning in life, and identity, then it is an idol. When an idol gets a grip on your heart, it spins out a whole set of false definitions of success, failure, happiness, and sadness. It redefines reality in terms of itself.*

Jesus.

I DIDN'T KNOW I WAS DEAD

Still on the fence about believing I needed to disassociate myself from the organization, I was advised to read a blog by Jessica Hines, a former AKA in my chapter. Her blog was about her denouncing as well.

This is a piece of her blog—

To Thee, O Alpha Kappa Alpha. We pledge our hearts, our minds and our strength. To foster thy teachings, obey thy laws and make Thee supreme service to all mankind. O Alpha Kappa Alpha We Greet Thee.

After, I heard the Holy Spirit say "MOCK".

So, I read it again and saw that the pledge was mocking the first commandment word for word.

In the text, a teacher asked Jesus what's the most important commandment, He answered:

Love the Lord your God with all your heart and with all your soul and with all your mind and with all your strength. The Second is this: Love your neighbor as yourself. There is no commandment greater than these.

Mark 12:29-31

I read her blog late at night and felt a darkness in my room and extremely uneasy as I reflected on all of the pledges and rituals we used to do and say. I woke up the next day knowing what I needed to do.

Everything that is good is not God. Just because Greek organizations do community service and other good things for the community, does not mean it's for Christ's followers. I gathered every piece of AKA item I had and I called my cousin Matthew. We went to our Aunt Tina and Uncle Pop's house, where there was a fire pit, and burned everything!

I had to break the covenant I made with that organization!

I instantly felt a sense of peace over me. I sent video messages to some of the women in my chapter informing them of my decision and a couple of months later, I wrote a blog about it. I spoke about my decision publicly to disassociate myself from the organization. Some people say it's not that deep, but that's our pride blinding us. And as I spoke about in the previous chapter, there are people looking up to us.

Who are you showing them?

*Don't love the world's ways. Don't love the world's goods.
Love of the world squeezes out love for the Father.
Practically everything that goes on in the world—wanting your
own way, wanting everything for yourself, **wanting to appear
important**—has nothing to do with the Father. **It just isolates
you from Him.** The world and all its wanting, wanting,
wanting is on the way out—but whoever does what God wants
is set for eternity.*

1 John 2:15-17 MSG

*Then, calling the crowd to join his disciples, he said, "If any
of you wants to be my follower, you must give up your own
way, take up your cross, and follow me. If you try to hang on
to your life, you will lose it. But if you give up your life for
my sake and for the sake of the Good News, you will save it.
And what do you benefit if you gain the whole world but
lose your own soul? Is anything worth more than your soul?
If anyone is ashamed of me and my message in these
adulterous and sinful days, the Son of Man will be ashamed
of that person when he returns in the glory of his Father with
the holy angels."*

Mark 8:34-38 NLT

Dying to myself, means being obedient to **all** The Lord tells
me to do even if it means looking crazy to others. Dying to
myself means making the continual decision so show others
Christ more than I show them myself. Dying to myself
means not just using my social media platforms to say, "Hey

63

look at me! I'm cute!" but "Hey, look at Christ! Narrow is the way!"

The more time I spent with Christ, the more He showed me what He wanted to do through me. The more He showed me, the more I had to die!

He's trying to show you what He wants to do in your life, too. What's hindering you from hearing him and obeying?

I once asked myself, "What am I doing, living in a hotel room? I could be home with my wife and my son!" And the Spirit of the Lord rose up in my spirit and said, "Dead men don't gripe." You know what happens to a living sacrifice? It dies. Dead men never fight back, either. . . .Dead men never get even. . . . Prophets must give up their bodies as a living sacrifice. Even today they throw stones at prophets. Some of you say, "Yes, I want the prophet's ministry." Will you still want it when things like this happen? Will you still be willing to "present your bodies a living sacrifice, holy, acceptable unto God, which is your reasonable service"?

Ed Dufresne The Prophet: Friend of God

Even if everyone rejects the message The Lord gives me to share...

Even when I no longer get invited on vacations with my friends...

I DIDN'T KNOW I WAS DEAD

Even if everyone is going one way and I'm going the opposite way...

Even when if I feel lonely at times walking such a narrow path...

Even if I get put in a box of being "Too Holy" ...

If God gets the glory, then so be it!

So put to death and deprive of power the evil longings of your earthly body [with its sensual, self-centered instincts] immorality, impurity, sinful passion, evil desire, and greed, which is [a kind of] idolatry [because it replaces your devotion to God].

Colossians 3:5 AMP

What is in your life that does not represent Christ?

Bitterness?

Envy?

Greed?

Unforgiveness?

Lust?

Idols?

Pride?

Sexual immorality?

Hate?

Ask yourself—have I died to myself?

If you said no, guess what? That's okay because dying to ourselves is a DAILY thing.

Pride can pop up inside of us because of an advancement.

Unforgiveness can quickly pop into our lives because of something hateful that someone did to us.

A gift from God can quickly turn into an idol if we desire it more than God.

This is why we must daily ask the Lord to cleanse us and purify us so that we are consecrated and ready to do the work of The Lord at all times!

1 Thessalonians 5:22-24 Amplified Bible says,

Abstain from every form of evil [withdraw and keep away from it]. Now may the God of peace Himself sanctify you through and through [that is, separate you from profane and vulgar things, make you pure and whole and undamaged—consecrated to Him—set apart for His purpose]; and may your spirit and soul and body be kept complete and [be found] blameless at the coming of our Lord Jesus Christ. Faithful and absolutely trustworthy is He who is calling you [to Himself for your salvation], and He will do it [He will fulfill His call by making you holy, guarding you, watching over you, and protecting you as His own].

Whoever does not take up their cross and follow me is not worthy of me.

Matthew 10:38 NIV

Pray

Lord, I thank You and I praise You for choosing me and setting me apart. Purify me Lord. Create in me a clean heart, O God; and renew a right spirit within me. (Psalm 51:10) Lord, thank You for Your grace and Your mercy. I desire, Lord, to live for You. Soften my heart Lord and show me things in my life that are not like You. Lord, I know that You desire what's best for me. Help me, Lord, to remain on the safe path You have set before me by being obedient to you. I thank You Lord for removing all types of evil from my life and replacing that evil with Your peace. Show me what is not like You Lord and give me the strength to refrain from it. I decree and declare that everything in my life that is keeping me from living wholeheartedly for You will be removed. I will be able to see the things in my life I have made idols. I will be able to see where I am bitter. I will be able to see when I am straying away from You. I thank You for eyes to see and for ears to hear from You. Make me more like You Lord. In Jesus Name, Amen.

I DIDN'T KNOW I WAS DEAD

I DIDN'T KNOW I WAS DEAD

CHAPTER SIX
SOCIAL MEDIA KILLS

For all these worldly things, these evil desires—the craze for sex, the ambition to buy everything that appeals to you, and the pride that comes from wealth and importance—these are not from God. They are from this evil world itself. And this world is fading away, and these evil, forbidden things will go with it, but whoever keeps doing the will of God will live forever.

1 John 2:16-17 Living Bible

The original temptation is still centered in these very things: the lust of the eyes, the lust of the flesh, and the boastful pride of life. As we yield to these false motives, we start erecting barriers around our eyes and our hands—the very tools God wants to use as receptacles for His great presence.

The Lifestyle of a Prophet

As I read this excerpt from the book, The Lifestyle of a Prophet by James W. Goll, I breathed a sigh of relief knowing my strong dislike for social media was not just from me, but from God. A five-minute scroll through my timeline is the most draining thing for me.

I can get on social media with all of the right intentions and leave wishing I was in a relationship, not feeling like I'm doing enough, wishing I was skinnier, wishing I was on vacation, wanting a lace front wig... the list goes on.

70

I DIDN'T KNOW I WAS DEAD

The Lust of the Eyes

Lust is defined as an intense desire or need, a craving.

Lust does not always have to be a sexual desire.

*Lust leads to sin. Sin leads to **Death.***

After lusting for what I just saw on social media, I began to take actions to satisfy my lust. Ordering weave from the site I just saw someone post even though I didn't have the money for it, starting a fad diet to lose weight fast because my friend just posted a photo in her bikini, and becoming unsatisfied with my business because it isn't flourishing like someone else's.

The weave I just bought, with the money I didn't have, was a waste because my edges broke out after having the sew-in installed for one week. Yes, seven days.

The body I just envied was photoshopped. I was comparing myself to something that was not real.

The business I envied was in serious debt.

True stories.

I was so frustrated as to why God put a hold on my finances, until He spoke to me so clearly and said, "Look at where you are spending your money". My priorities were ALL messed up. I had thousands of dollars in debt on credit cards yet chose to drop $350 on some weave that I wore for one week, spent over $400 at a nutrition center to begin a fad diet that I stayed on for one week, and spent more money on new items for my business instead of selling what I already had. After I calculated all the money I spent on unnecessary things, The Lord revealed to me that one of my credit cards could have been paid off in full if I had chosen to use my financial resources on that. Wow!

When I looked deeper into the root of why I lusted after all of the unnecessary things I had just spent my money on, it was from what I was continually absorbing from social media. If we are not disciplined in what we take in through our eye gate, we will not be disciplined in any other area of our life.

Matthew 6:22-23 New Living Translation says,

> *Your eye is like a lamp that provides light for your body. When your eye is healthy, your whole body is filled with light. But when your eye is unhealthy, your whole body is filled with darkness. And if the light you think you have is actually darkness, how deep that darkness is!*

I DIDN'T KNOW I WAS DEAD

Social media is just one example of how we easily begin to take in too much with our eyes. We need to control who we follow, we need to control how much time we spend on each platform, and we need to control what conversations we entertain.

In case you didn't know, social media is misleading.

What we see on social media is only partial truth, if it's any truth at all.

On social media we have the ability to post whatever our heart desires. We can post photos from weeks ago, months ago, or years ago, all while sitting in our beds crying and discontent with life... only in hopes to show the world we're good. We can type whatever we want in our bio to make us seem important. We can write and share whatever we want, while omitting what we choose.

I say all this because social media was my friend in hiding what I didn't want people to know.

My bio changed every week, and if I could put them all together it looked something like this:

RN. BSN.

#livtoshoot

Dancer

AKA 1908

World Traveler

Philippians 4:13

She believed she could so she did...

Although all of these things were true, I chose not to mention, being depressed, searching for something, not happy with my career, in an abusive relationship...

Instead, I found some nice motivational quotes on Pinterest to post and flexed every time I went on vacation.

On social media, I was living my best life!

The Lust of the Flesh
The strong desire or craving to please our flesh.

Social media is a breeding ground for the love of this world. Social media glorifies all of what is opposite of the love of Christ. Just look at the things that go viral. Look at the pages with the most followers or the content that is most popular.

What do you see?

Posting a photo half naked will get you way more attention than posting a photo about Jesus!

When we desire attention is when we give into vain images of ourselves for the pleasure of people. When we see our friends or others getting attention from over sexualizing themselves, our flesh wants to do the same because as fleshly humans, we naturally want that attention.

We were made to be loved and nothing is wrong with it! Our desire to be loved becomes an issue when we desire love and acceptance from people before our Heavenly Father. Once we want other's acceptance is when we are lusting after our own fleshly desires. Pleasing our flesh is the opposite of pleasing our spirit man.

Romans 8:5 Amplified Bible says,

> *For those who are living according to the flesh set their minds on the things of the flesh [which gratify the body], but those who are living according to the Spirit, [set their minds on] the things of the Spirit [His will and purpose].*

I knew what outfits to buy to get more double taps. I knew what photos and videos would get the attention of men I wanted to notice me. I knew what to post to piss my boyfriend off when I went out of town. I knew exactly how to give my flesh what she wanted.

And for those of us that think we can play with fire and not get burned, desiring to satisfy our flesh through social media can lead us into sin we never imagined we'd be in.

James 1:14-15 New Living Translation says,

Temptation comes from our own desires, which entice us and drag us away. These desires give birth to sinful actions. And when sin is allowed to grow, it gives birth to death.

Be mindful of what or who you are attracting by what you say, what you post, and how you move. Who or what are you inviting into your life on your platforms? Do your platforms point people to Christ, yourself, or Satan? Is what you see drawing you to Christ, yourself, or Satan?

The Pride of Life

I am naturally ambitious, and it wasn't until recently that I realized ambition is not of God.

I DIDN'T KNOW I WAS DEAD

Webster defines ambition as, an ardent desire for rank, fame, or power. The desire to achieve a particular end.

The Lord killed my ambition.

Social media ignites our desire to be ambitions. The bible says in Luke when Satan tempted Jesus,

Then he led Jesus up [to a high mountain] and displayed before Him all the kingdoms of the inhabited earth [and their magnificence] in the twinkling of an eye. And the devil said to Him, "I will give You all this realm and its glory [its power, its renown]; because it has been handed over to me, and I give it to whomever I wish. Therefore if You worship before me, it will all be Yours." Jesus replied to him, "It is written and forever remains written, 'You shall worship the Lord your God and serve only Him.'

Luke 4:5-8 AMP

Social media's definition of living is not the same as Christ's.

The enemy wants us to look at all the world has to offer us and bow to him in order to achieve it. We see people with power, titles, relationships, money, and many other things and wish to have what they have. That alone by itself is not bad. But, when we attempt to achieve these things apart from Christ, or desire them more than Christ, they are idols!

77

I DIDN'T KNOW I WAS DEAD

The bible tells us in Matthew 6:33, New Living Translation,

> *Seek the Kingdom of God above all else, and live*
> *righteously, and he will give you everything you need.*

There are so many voices on social media pointing in different directions. If we are not disciplined, we will end up going in the wrong direction due to listening to the wrong voice.

We are quick to follow the person with millions of dollars because, we desire millions of dollars. But, what if your millions of dollars will come through the book you write only by spending time with God?

We are so quick to follow the entrepreneur who created multiple successful businesses. But, what if your business is not supposed to look like anyone else's? You would only know what it's supposed to look like by a revelation from God through prayer.

We are so quick to want to please people with a bunch of followers on social media, because we believe they will be our next big break to achieve more. But, what if the person

78

who is going to open the next God-given door in your life has 35 followers and you've been ignoring them?

We are so quick to post what we believe other people want to see like our achievements and our successes. But, what if the testimony you never wanted to share was what would not only set you apart from everyone else, but would save the souls of many?

Instead of worrying about how many people follow you, think about the message you are giving those who already follow you. What do they see?

Matthew 7:13-14 The Message Bible says,
Don't look for shortcuts to God. The market is flooded with surefire, easygoing formulas for a successful life that can be practiced in your spare time. Don't fall for that stuff, even though crowds of people do. The way to life—to God!—is vigorous and requires total attention.

The way to LIFE is the way to God!

It is vigorous and requires TOTAL attention.

Want to live? Take a break from social media and give your total attention to God. It's amazing that spending intentional time with The Lord destroyed everything I thought I knew about success. Our lives are unique and are not like anyone else's. We can't follow some easy-going formula for overnight success, that's not real. Seeking God's will for our lives is how we will succeed.

Social media can be used for good, but pray for discipline and discernment to recognize distractions.

Be set apart on social media too!

Best believe social media is a breeding ground for attacks from the enemy. Pettiness and people throwing shots, rather subliminally or not, is nothing but a distraction.

The unfollow button is your friend.

Protect your peace on social media too!

I DIDN'T KNOW I WAS DEAD

CHAPTER SEVEN
PEOPLE PLEASING KILLS

If pleasing other people becomes the goal, you will spend the rest of your life trying to satisfy and you'll never have peace.
Bishop T.D. Jakes

What is your why?

Do you know it?

Why do you do what you do?

Why do you move the way you move?

Why did you start that business?

Why did you start your ministry?

Why do you post what you post?

Why do you say what you say?

Why do you pursue what you pursue?

For you?

Who's influencing your decisions?

Are you happy?

Who or what is in control of your joy?

If it's not people, then why do you quit when they don't approve?

Why do you go harder when they applaud?

You don't?

Are you sure...?

My people-pleasing resume is pretty legit. I would definitely qualify for the highest paid people-pleasing job because I was your number one, "Yes" girl. I've gotten better at saying "No", but, I still may go through condemnation afterwards. You see, being a helper and a giver is my nature. It took me maturing to realize that helping people does not mean giving them what they want. Helping people may be denying them what they want, to give them what they need.

So, why do we please people?
1. Fear of letting someone down
2. Fear of not being liked or accepted
3. Fear of criticism
4. Fear of rejection
5. Fear of not being in control

...FEAR. (False evidence appearing real)

I DIDN'T KNOW I WAS DEAD

In my head, I tend to make up scenarios.
The "what ifs".
My mind definitely wonders.

I begin to think: what if I spoke like this, wore this, did this...
will they like me?
What if I posted this, what would they say?
What if I didn't post that, what would they say?
What if I unfollowed everyone, what would they think?

We all do this.

The danger is when those "what ifs", "what will they think",
and "what will they say", begin to weigh so heavy that we get
stuck.

We worry so much that we don't move.

Today, I want you to begin to think differently. You have to.
People will always think something about you! Good
thoughts or bad thoughts! The ones who are the most critical
most likely are stuck due to what others will think of them,
so they have nothing better to do than to criticize you
negatively.

Prior to every major leap of faith, I am bombarded with the "what ifs" and fear of what people will think or say. It's going to happen to you, too. That's why, personally, I move silently. I don't announce what I'm doing publicly until it is time to release whatever I'm doing. I don't ask the public, "What would you all think if I did this?" "What would you all think if I dyed my hair orange?" "Should I write a book?" "Should I start a clothing store?" "Should I start a blog?" "Which book cover do you like best?"

If the Lord told us to do it, why are we seeking validation from everyone else?

I ask questions in private to my close family members or friends. I trust that they have my best interest in heart and will provide the feedback I need. For example, when I was working on my book cover, I showed my parents, grandmother, and cousin the cover and asked for their feedback about what I needed to change. I didn't ask social media.

I wonder how many things you decided not to do because you asked everyone and their mom, and someone shut your idea down.

"There's no way you can do that."

"You're crazy to think you would do well."

"No one would read your book because no one knows you."

"That's not your lane."

"You aren't qualified."

Or maybe no one told you that, but you told yourself that.

Tell your inner critic to shut up too!

I have to tell the perfectionist in my head to shut up constantly. She's so annoying.

Another danger is when those "what ifs", "what will people say", "what will people think", begin to weigh so heavy that you become disobedient to God.

God- "Olivia, do business with so and so. She needs an encounter with Me and I'm using you."
Me- "Um, Lord. What will everyone think about me publicly working with her? She's into witchcraft and..."

God- "Olivia... she needs an encounter with Me. It's not about what other people think."

For we speak as messengers approved by God to be entrusted with the Good News. Our purpose is to please God, not people. He alone examines the motives of our hearts.

1 Thessalonians 2:4 NLT

As messengers of the gospel, people may look at you funny in regards to who you speak to, or who you choose to hang around, but only God can examine the motive of your heart. If your motive is to bring certain people to Christ, it doesn't matter what other people think. Who the Lord assigns to us may be different than someone else. Just make sure if you are going into secular territories, you, are MATURE in your walk so that you do not fall.

Don't delay or be disobedient to your assignment because you want to please man.

Fearing people is a dangerous trap, but trusting the Lord means safety.

Proverbs 29:25 NLT

I realized after coming home to Christ, I never wanted to be all the way in because of what people would think of me. I didn't want to be that church girl that was too holy. But the reality is, people see me that way now and that's fine with me. Because I know the truth, I have to walk in truth. Trying

to be half way in the world and half way in the church got me
snatched into the world and in a bunch of mess.

If you are playing the fence, wanting to please God and
people, I pray you make the choice today to repent and
surrender. It's dangerous for those of us who know better to
not do what's right. Your soul is worth more than what other
people think, say, or feel.

*So any person who knows what is right to do but does not
do it, to him it is sin.*
James 4:17 AMP

We have to be God pleasers, not people pleasers.
How do we obtain enough courage to stand up for what is
Godly, instead of bowing to the desires of men?

Walking by The Spirit
*But I say, walk and live [habitually] in the [Holy] Spirit
[responsive to and controlled and guided by the Spirit]; then
you will certainly not gratify the cravings and desires of the
flesh (of human nature without God).*
Galatians 5:16 AMP

*But the fruit of the Spirit is love, joy, peace, longsuffering,
gentleness, goodness, faith,*
Galatians 5:22 KJV

Prayer/Communication with God

Watch and pray so that you will not fall into temptation. The spirit is willing, but the flesh is weak.
Matthew 26:41 NIV

And the Holy Spirit helps us in our weakness. For example, we don't know what God wants us to pray for, but the Holy Spirit prays for us with groanings that cannot be expressed in words.
Romans 8:26 NLT

Staying Ready

Remain in me, and I will remain in you. For a branch cannot produce fruit if it is severed from the vine, and you cannot be fruitful unless you remain in me.

John 15:4 NLT

Therefore, put on the complete armor of God, so that you will be able to [successfully] resist and stand your ground in the evil day [of danger], and having done everything [that the crisis demands], to stand firm [in your place, fully prepared, immovable, victorious]. So stand firm and hold your ground, having tightened the wide band of truth (personal integrity, moral courage) around your waist and having put on the breastplate of righteousness (an upright heart), and having strapped on your feet the gospel of peace in preparation [to face the enemy with firm-footed stability and the readiness produced by the good news]. Above all, lift up the [protective] shield of faith with which you can extinguish all the flaming arrows of the evil one. And take the helmet of salvation, and the sword of the Spirit, which is the Word of God. With all prayer and petition pray [with specific requests] at all times [on every occasion and in every season] in the Spirit, and with this in view, stay alert with all

perseverance and petition [interceding in prayer] for
all God's people.
Ephesians 6:13-18 AMP

Choosing not to be a people pleaser is not easy. All of those things you may fear, like persecution and being isolated, may happen. But, all of those things happened to Jesus during His walk on earth. Jesus will reward our obedience to do what is right.

> *Blessed [comforted by inner peace and God's love] are those who are persecuted for doing that which is morally right, for theirs is the kingdom of heaven [both now and forever]. Blessed [morally courageous and spiritually alive with life-joy in God's goodness] are you when people insult you and persecute you, and falsely say all kinds of evil things against you because of [your association with] Me. Be glad and exceedingly joyful, for your reward in heaven is great [absolutely inexhaustible]; for in this same way they persecuted the prophets who were before you.*
> Matthew 5:10-12 AMP

I believe you can stop being a people pleaser. I pray you believe you can too. Every day it's a choice not to bow to the opinions of man, but to stay connected with Christ and stay set apart. Choosing to do Godly things may make you look weird, but I'll be weird with you! After 26 years of my life pleasing others, I didn't feel complete freedom until I asked The Lord to show me every area of my life where I was trying to please people and not Him.

I was shocked to see even when I started my business, Can We Live, that I was trying to please "church people". I wanted to make sure my business was acceptable for their religious standards, and almost forgot that I'm not supposed to be afraid of working with secular businesses or people with different beliefs as me. What Can We Live has is what they need! Jesus. Wanting to form this Christian clique was NOT God's plan for Can We Live. I'm so thankful He showed me what was happening within a month of the shop being open. I quickly repented and remembered a Church hired ME when I was not walking with Christ. Let us be God pleasers and not people pleasers. That includes wanting to please the church people over wanting to please Christ.

Ask yourself, is this me?

Pray

Father God, help me to recognize when I am attempting to please people and not You. Show me where I lack the boldness to stand up for what it is right. Holy Spirit, lead me and guide me. Father God, give me Your strength. I desire to live for You and to please You, not man. Help me to remain set a part, and to live freely for you and you alone. In Jesus Name, Amen.

Obviously, I'm not trying to win the approval of people, but of God. If pleasing people were my goal, I would not be Christ's servant.

Galatians 1:10 NLT

I DIDN'T KNOW I WAS DEAD

CHAPTER EIGHT

INSECURITY KILLS

I haven't been at peace for a while now & I just haven't been myself, lately. I've been praying about it because it's really been taking a toll on me & my heart has been heavy. I've been ignoring something I've had an issue with for a while now & it makes sense to why I'm always temporarily happy with you. Which is your lusty spirit. It genuinely makes me sick to my stomach how freely you talk about sex & other women. You can freely say things like Cali women have the best sex & that you've done your individual research. Or how I can fall asleep on your shoulder & in the meantime you are liking other girl's pics from weeks ago. Or how you discuss different women you want based on their physical features. Or how you feed into women's thirst traps regardless of my feelings. I've just realized I will never satisfy you. Because lust is never satisfied & lust will eventually run out. I just realized I'm settling & I've let go of my standards & I'm way better than that. You would say you want me to trust you & be submissive to you when you blatantly tell me, to my face, that you have eyes for other women. I'm not naive nor insecure when it comes to other women. There will always be someone colder than I am or with a better body & we both know that... but it's way deeper than that. I'm not trying to wait around for you to change or have some respect for the fact you're having sex with me but say the most disrespectful things on social networks. I can't take it anymore. & I won't. I wish I would've never let things get so deep because then it wouldn't have hurt as much. I don't want to keep pretending this is what I want. You said yourself that if I ever needed something serious to not call you because you aren't reliable...

Words I never said. -January 16, 2015

94

I DIDN'T KNOW I WAS DEAD

I thought I was done. I knew I deserved better. I had written it out and was ready to send it but I didn't. Why? Why did I put up with this? My friends and family told me I deserved better, that I could have any man I wanted to have, but I didn't believe them. Why?

Insecurity Kills.

As I read back on that note I saved in my phone, I was shocked all over again. It's extremely easy for me to get caught up in who I am now that I can sometimes forget who I was, and what I put up with. The Olivia now would have told herself, girl you're bugging... But the reality is, the Olivia then told herself that too. I knew what I was putting up with was pitiful and I knew I felt some type of way or I would've never written that note. Yet, I just couldn't take my own advice and send it.

What was it about me that didn't believe I deserved better? What did I lack that kept me entering the same cycles over and over again?

I would answer "confidence", but that's not the only answer.

I was extremely confident, well I thought I was, before entering that relationship.

The answer was that I lacked protection.

The definition of Insecurity is:
1. The uncertainty or anxiety about oneself; lack of confidence and

2. The state of being open to danger or threat; lack of protection

Insecurity is not just about lacking confidence. Insecurity is about being open to dangers. What I was missing was protection, my covering, which is a relationship with Jesus Christ.

If I had filled the void of wanting to be loved by a man with Jesus and truly sought God, I would have seen all of the red flags that I missed before getting too deeply involved in the relationships I chose in my life. That's why it's so dangerous to be discontent in our seasons of singleness. Wanting to rush out of that season in the pursuit of having someone is breeding ground for the enemy. He is waiting for someone vulnerable who lacks wisdom and patience.

It's easy to hide our insecurities, and some of us don't even realize we are hiding them. Some of us don't realize we have replaced God (our protection) with other things...

Our titles
Our relationships
Our money
Our degrees
Our jobs
Our talents

We hide.

If your title, Doctor, got stripped away from you, would you still have purpose?
If your relationship ended, would you still have confidence?
If your money got taken, would you still feel stable?
If your big six-bedroom house where your friends love to come visit was gone, would you still feel loved?
If you got injured and could no longer play professional football, would you still feel worthy?

Or, are you insecure?

Our security does not come from these things. These things are all temporary and can, and will, be taken from us.

For all that is in the world—the lust of the flesh [craving for sensual gratification] and the lust of the eyes [greedy longings of the mind] and the pride of life [assurance in one's own resources or in the stability of earthly things]—these do not come from the Father but are from the world [itself].

And the world passes away and disappears, and with it the forbidden cravings (the passionate desires, the lust) of it; but he who does the will of God and carries out His purposes in his life abides (remains) forever.

1 John 2:16-17 AMP

Just because The Lord allows things to happen in your life doesn't mean it is His Divine will for you. A lot of the things we have started in life were because we wanted it, not necessarily that God wanted it for us. A lot of people we choose to date and/or marry, may be who we wanted, but were not God's divine person for us. Don't settle for His permissive will by choosing to strive after everything you believe you need in life to be secure. Rest completely in Him. Allow Him to show you what steps to take to do what He is calling you to do. And remember, God looks at people different than humans do. We may look at someone with their doctorate degree and believe they are the best fit for a platform, but God may look at someone with a high school diploma and Christ-like character and say "No I want her instead". If God is calling you to a position, He will put you there. Don't go striving after what you believe you need without the Lord's direction.

> But God told Samuel, "Looks aren't everything. Don't be impressed with his looks and stature. I've already eliminated him. God judges persons differently than humans do. Men and women look at the face; God looks into the heart."
>
> 1 Samuel 16:7 MSG

Declare— God made no mistakes when He made me. I am able to do all of the things God is calling me to do. I am not insecure. I lack nothing without Him. I will not settle for God's permissive will, instead I will pursue God's divine will for my life. I am loved. I am protected. I am whole.

Pray— Lord, reveal to me the things in my life that I have chosen over You. Forgive me for putting my hope in earthly things instead of completely trusting You with Lordship over my life. You are Lord and You are God all by Yourself. Help me to walk in agreement of what I just spoke and follow You alone, not the things of this world. Keep me in Your perfect peace and continue to watch over me and protect me. In Jesus Name, Amen.

This is the confidence we have in approaching God: that if we ask anything according to his will, he hears us.

1 John 5:14 NIV

I DIDN'T KNOW I WAS DEAD

CHAPTER NINE

PERFECTIONISM KILLS

The truth is, for the longest I've been scared of being honest. Scared to admit that it was deeper than my feelings getting hurt or my heart being broken. I was scared to let the world know that even on the outside when everyone saw this strong, goal-driven, & well-rounded woman, inside hid an insecure female that for years never felt good enough. You'd be surprised how well I hid hurt behind my smile & big cheeks.
Words I never said. -October 31, 2014

When I was in a leadership development program, I had to sit down with my mentor and go over my 360 emotional intelligence assessments. A 360 emotional intelligence assessment is when you rate how you perceive yourself and other people rate how they perceive you. I had to provide 20 people, five in four different categories including family, friends, colleagues, and community. I normally struggle with constructive criticism because I beat myself up enough; so hearing others criticism on top of my own was not something I was looking forward to.

Nevertheless, when we started off reviewing the assessment I was pretty pleased to see that everyone either saw me better than how I saw myself, or agreed with me! No bad ratings I thought!! Then, I got to the comment section...

'What should Olivia start doing... stop doing... ect.'

I began to read the constructive criticism, which to me just looked like a bunch of hateful things to say, and slowly felt myself sink back into my chair. My mind couldn't even remember the positive feedback I just read. I felt myself wanting to fall back, as I often do, when something becomes uncomfortable. My mentor began to ask me my thoughts, and I could barely respond because I was fighting back tears.

When I left the meeting, I cried in my car and my mind was consumed with wondering who said what.

Then I began to think...

How often do I choose to "fall back" from something that makes me dig deeper into why I am feeling a certain way, instead of facing it head on and dealing with it?

Perfectionism is crippling, a very unrealistic, and damaging goal to have for ourselves. It wasn't others criticism that made me sink... it was me. Me realizing I missed that unrealistic bar, again. Me realizing I'd never measure up to the standard I STILL had for myself.

Their honesty showed me they desired for me to continue to grow and mature into who The Lord was calling me to be. In order for that to happen, and to continue to happen, I had to learn to take constructive feedback, not run from it!

Perfectionism is defined by Merriam- Webster as a disposition to regard anything short of perfection as unacceptable.

That's how my brain was set up. Not perfect means I failed.

Jesus doesn't ask us to be perfect, but He does ask that we mature.

I had to learn to accept God's grace as I continue to grow...

I pray you do too...

When the Lord revealed to me that I needed to write this book, I decided to rent a hotel in Dublin, OH for the weekend and just get away. This is my first book so I wasn't quite sure how writing would go, but I just knew in my head I needed to fast the entire time I was writing. Who told me that? No one, other than the perfectionist in my head trying to be super spiritual. So, I went on my trip, didn't eat anything the first day, and let's just say I was **MISERABLE**. I remember calling my grandmother and she said I sounded bored. I was so confused on why I was at this hotel all by myself, lonely, hungry, and irritated. Now don't get me wrong, I've fasted before and usually when The Lord calls me to fast, it's not a struggle, but He gives me grace to fast. My grandmother began to tell me that she used to take trips by herself all the time to just get away and spend time with the Lord. She said she would go to all these nice fancy restaurants, stay at nice hotels, and would come back home so refreshed.

I began thinking well that sounds way better than what I'm doing...

I got a lot of studying and reading done as I was consecrating myself the first day, but my creativity was just not flowing. I woke up the next morning praying and I kid you not, The Lord said, "You told yourself not to eat, not me".

Oh... lol.

I thankfully and quickly, went to the Bob Evans that was across the street and ate. I ended up going for a walk that day at this park, read about 3-4 books, made an outline for this book, and sat by the pool to relax. It was such a productive and peaceful day. Thank God I stopped trying to be extra perfect and just ate.

The third day I was there, God said, Olivia where would you want the guy you're dating to take you tonight? I thought, well ice cream sounds good! Well let's go get ice cream, said The Lord! On the way to get ice cream, I literally cried my eyes out because God spoke to me so clearly in this moment.

He said,

Olivia, I want what you want. I want you to be happy and I want to give you the desires of your heart. I loved you the same when you were in your mess the same as I love you now. Nothing you strive to do will make me love you more or anything you don't do will make me love you less.

106

It took a trip to get ice cream, to hear The Lord clear as day. Not me trying to be extra perfect out in the middle of nowhere by myself.

Perfectionism is so heavy.

When we strive to be perfect, we are not accepting of God's grace.

For no one can ever be made right with God by doing what the law commands. The law simply shows us how sinful we are. But now God has shown us a way to be made right with him without keeping the requirements of the law, as was promised in the writings of Moses and the prophets long ago. We are made right with God by placing our faith in Jesus Christ. And this is true for everyone who believes, no matter who we are. For everyone has sinned; we all fall short of God's glorious standard. Yet God, in his grace, freely makes us right in his sight. He did this through Christ Jesus when he freed us from the penalty for our sins.

Romans 3:20-24 NLT

We are FREE. Not because of works, but because of Jesus dying on the cross for our sins.

Pray

Lord, I thank You and I praise You for Your grace. Today I accept the grace You so freely want to give to me. Lord, You are perfect, not me. Help me to continue to mature so that I may be prepared to do all that You are calling me to do. As I mature I pray that You show me when I am being hard on myself. Help me to love myself like You do, Lord. Thank You for being an amazing example. I thank You and praise You for lifting the burden of perfectionism off of me in this very moment. I love You God. In Jesus Name, Amen.

I DIDN'T KNOW I WAS DEAD

CHAPTER TEN

BUSYNESS KILLS

Most days I become overwhelmed very easily. I get into these spaces where I think about all the things I have to do, I completely shut down, decide to go to sleep, and just try again tomorrow. I start thinking to myself- maybe I'm doing too much. Trying to balance working 40 hours a week, running this new business, teaching dance, trying to eat healthy, working out, getting enough sleep, keeping my house clean, reading my bible, texting people back, making time for my loved ones, trying to have a social life, having me time... needless to say a lot of these things don't happen. I'm having difficulty finding balance. Recently I've been so tired and fatigued that I had to make a doctor's appointment to figure out what's really happening.

Words I never said. -November 11, 2016

The doctor wasn't who I needed. My life was on overdrive and I attempted to navigate without The Lord's direction. Not to mention, my life did not consist of consistent prayer, so I was just winging it.

Foolishly-

Busy.

Merriam-Webster defines busy as,

- engaged in action: OCCUPIED

- being in use
- full of activity: BUSTLING
- foolishly or intrusively active: MEDDLING
- full of distracting detail

Do you know that busyness can kill purpose if we are not careful?

We can fill our schedules with a bunch of distractions and believe we are doing what we are supposed to be doing. When in reality, we end up becoming too tired and overwhelmed when it's time to focus on what God initially wanted us to do.

This book should be titled, I Didn't Know I Was Dead... written by The Queen of Busy.

I didn't get the revelation that busyness kills until 2018. I spent 25 years of my life filling up my schedule and trying to hustle, impress people, and strive for success. I learned, it is during those still quiet moments that I'm able to hear clearly from God for the direction of my life. We need His direction daily, so making the mindful choice of penciling in those still quiet moments in our schedules is so necessary.

I believe our need for busyness is rooted in fear and control.

Fear of telling others "no" when our schedules are already full.
Fear of missing out on something.
Fear of not doing enough.
Lack of trust in God's timing.
Wanting to be in control of our own schedules.

I'm bossy. That's just how I was made. I believe that's why The Lord gave me businesses, it's my strong point to be the boss. But my issue is when I try to be the boss over God. He kindly reminds me, by canceling my plans at times, that He is in control, not me.

I remember one weekend I had four photoshoots scheduled that were all outside and rain was not in the forecast. Yet, when the weekend came, what happened? It rained and every single shoot had to be rescheduled. God? I needed that money!

No daughter, you need to spend time with me!!!

Throws mini temper tantrum

Instead, that weekend was spent inside the house reading a book and asking God what He desired for me to do. Him cancelling my plans happens frequently, actually. At first it was quite annoying because I refused to surrender control over my schedule, but now I'm thankful He cancels things for me. I don't realize I need it until after I sit my butt down and reflect that what I scheduled for myself was pretty unrealistic.

Time management isn't really my thing. I look at the calendar and see an open hour like "yup, I have time". When in reality I forgot to pencil in eating or just sitting down and taking a breath for five minutes. That's why The Lord is so gracious and just cancels stuff for me when I'm doing too much.

Being disciplined in stewarding our time is necessary in order to be successful in what The Lord is calling us to do. We have to use wisdom in our schedules and our commitments.

Seek the Lord's guidance and will.

Look carefully then how you walk, not as unwise but as wise, making the best use of the time, because the days are evil.

I DIDN'T KNOW I WAS DEAD

Therefore do not be foolish, but understand what the will of the Lord is.

Ephesians 5:15-17 ESV

Bishop LaFayette Scales said,

I can tell you where you'll be five years from now by the books you read, how you spend your time, and who you spend your time with.

The Lord wants us to seek His will and make the best use of our time. God sees time different than we do. What we may believe we need now, The Lord is like, "no you're good". And what we may believe we need to wait and do The Lord is like, "nope do this NOW". But, how do we know what He wants from us in this season? By communicating with Him.

Pastor Tony Ransom explained communication so well one service at Rhema Christian Center. He said communication is not just saying everything we want to say and then leaving the room and slamming the door. No, communication is saying what we need to say and then stopping and listening to hear what the other person has to say. This applies to our communication with God as well. We have to stop talking and listen to what The Lord is saying.

Quiet your busy mind and renew your thinking in regards to what needs to be done in your life by your own efforts. God is trying to move in your life, yet you aren't allowing Him to by filling up your schedule with what you want to do. Surrender your time, your striving, and your high expectations of yourself and allow God to be God, and you to be His child.

The Lord showed me that it was time for me to go part-time at my full-time job at the hospital as a registered nurse. Now, I really had to pray to see if it was Him telling me this, because the way my bank account was set up... I needed that full-time check money.

Yet the Lord showed me I was way too busy and some choices needed to be made. One of those choices being to drop down to 24 hours a week. The Lord was trying to increase my clientele in business, but I was too busy with my full-time job to edit the photos I was taking over the weekend. The Lord also told me I needed to write this book and I honestly didn't have much time to sit down, while not being too tired to write it.

I was working 32 hours a week at Children's Hospital Primary Care Clinics, I was teaching dance class to students ages 5-15, I was running Olivia Kristin Photography, Can We Live, and Your Wedding Creatives. I was dancing in the dance ministry at church, taking a leadership course, attempting to be a good family member and friend, the list goes on and on... Let's just say I had way too many commitments.

In my leadership development program NXGEN, my mentor Ms. Lynette, constantly encouraged me to discover my Noble Goal in life. Basically, what was I put on this earth to do. She explained it was something bigger than me, something that couldn't just be obtained by me, and that would still be needed when I was no longer here. After months I finally came up with my Noble Goal:

To share truth in a creative
and nonconforming way.

I believe my purpose in life is to use my creativity, whether that's through writing, dancing, photography, or any other business the Lord may give me, to share Jesus and His light, wisdom, direction, and purpose with others.

After realizing this was my purpose in life, it made it easier to make the decision to go part-time and spend more time on the things where I knew The Lord wanted to use me. Now, quitting my job altogether would have been unwise. I see so many people going out on a limb to just quit their full-time job with benefits to pursue a dream. I support people stepping out on faith, but before "stepping out on faith" ask yourself these questions:

1. Is it what I want to do, or what The Lord is asking me to do?

2. Does it make sense? (If I quit my job, will I have money to pay my bills? Will I have health insurance? Will I be able to support my family)?

God doesn't ask us to do things that are unwise. Seek guidance from a respected mentor or Pastor before making any major life decisions.

Nevertheless, after reviewing all of my options and calculating bills, I realized I was able to live off of a part time salary. Now, maybe not live how I was living and spending a bunch of money on food, my nails, my lashes, waxing, and clothes. But, I was able to survive, take care of the necessities, and trust God to provide the rest.

After a couple of months into my new schedule I knew switching to part-time when I did was exactly what I was supposed to do. I had the adequate amount of time to edit photos, to spend time with Jesus, to write this book, and to do the things I was procrastinating doing with my businesses.

I made some cut backs in my spending and switched to a little more frugal lifestyle, but it was all worth it in that particular season. I will be honest and say sometimes I had just enough to pay my bills, and sometimes random expenses came, like needing a filling at the dentist or something for my car, but The Lord took care of it and has not let me down.

Trusting God with our schedules and our time, even when it doesn't make sense, is faith. We have to believe that He will take care of our every need when He asks us to do something. He wants us to rest, not to live a life striving and being foolishly busy. He desires for us to be purposeful, not just going through the motions of life.

The Lord is my Shepherd [to feed, to guide and to shield me], I shall not want. He lets me lie down in green pastures; He leads me beside the still and quiet waters. He refreshes and restores my soul (life); He leads me in the paths of righteousness for His name's sake.
Psalm 23:1-3 AMP

Pray

Lord, I desire to be purposeful, not just busy. I know that it is easy to be pulled in a lot of different directions. Lord, I release the fear of missing out, of letting someone down, or not doing enough over to You. Father, I desire to hear Your voice over any other when it comes to my schedule. Forgive me Lord for going to my e-mail or my social media accounts before I speak to You in the morning. Show me where I am distracted, show me where I have lost focus, and show me what I need to do in this season. Lord, I thank You that I don't need to worry about my schedule because I surrender it over to You. Reveal to me what needs to go and is taking too much time away from doing what You desire for me to do. I thank You for giving me the courage to say "no" and for Your peace as I become obedient to stewarding my time wisely. In Jesus Name, Amen.

It's useless to rise up early and go to bed late and work your worried fingers to the bone. Don't you know he enjoys giving rest to those he loves?

Psalm 127:2 MSG

CHAPTER ELEVEN
IGNORANCE KILLS

My people are destroyed for lack of knowledge...
Hosea 4:6

I spoke to a group of young girls at First Church of God one Sunday along with a couple of my coworkers from Nationwide Children's Hospital. My assignment was to discuss healthy dating and relationships, how to respond to peer pressure about being intimate, and to facilitate a discussion about teen's personal experiences with dating. I began with an icebreaker by asking a series of questions. I asked that they raise their thumbs up sign if they thought the scenario was cute or raise their thumbs down sign if they thought the scenario was toxic. For this specific presentation, I was speaking to young girls, but all of this applies to both men and women. If I was speaking to a group of boys or men, I would change the context.

The questions were as follows:
1. Your boyfriend texts you five times in a row, asking what you are doing and where you are
2. Your boyfriend always picks where you two hang out

3. Your boyfriend waits for you after practice every day, so he can walk you home

4. Your boyfriend buys you flowers after a fight

5. Your boyfriend gets mad when you like another boy's photo on Instagram

6. You boyfriend tells you he can't live without you

7. Your boyfriend jokingly says he'll slap you if he ever finds out you're cheating on him

8. Your boyfriend blocks all the male contacts in your phone

9. Your boyfriend chokes you while he kisses you

10. Your boyfriend wants you to change for him

11. Your goals become your boyfriend's goals. He now wants to go to the same college as you

12. Your boyfriend checks your Instagram DM's

13. Your boyfriend wants his name in your bio

14. Your boyfriend publicly tells you he loves you

15. Your boyfriend says he'll break up with you if you don't listen to him more

What do you think? Cute or toxic?

We laughed together and discussed each scenario in regards to if we thought it was cute, or if we thought it was toxic. I was blown away by the discernment of these young ladies, because I definitely lacked it. Some of these scenarios are easily distinguishable as toxic situations, but others are not. For instance, your boyfriend waits for you after practice so he can walk you home. That's so cute right? I think so! I switched it up a bit and asked, but what if you told him you want to walk home with your friends instead, but he continued to show up every day? Because he loves you and he just wants to make sure you get to your destination safely... Because he doesn't trust your friends walking with you. Is it still cute?

This led us into a discussion about toxic versus healthy relationships.

I asked, what are signs of toxic relationships?

- Controlling behavior- One partner makes all the decisions and tells the other what to do, what to wear, or who to spend time with. He or she is unreasonably jealous, and/or tries to isolate the partner from his or her friends and family
- Hostility- One dating partner picks a fight with or antagonizes the other partner
- Dishonesty
- Disrespect

- Dependence
- Intimidation- "threaten to break up"
- Physical violence
- Sexual violence
- Emotional abuse

What are signs of healthy relationships?

- Trust
- Boundaries
- Mutual Respect – each person values who the person is and understands the other person's boundaries
- Honesty- builds trust and strengthens the relationship
- Compromise- in a dating relationship each partner does not always get his or her way. Each should acknowledge different points of view and be willing to give and take
- Individuality- neither partner should have to compromise who he/she is, and his/her identity should not be based on the partner's identity. Each should continue seeing his or her friends doing the things he/she loves. Each should be supportive of

his/her partner wanting to pursue new hobbies or make new friends

- Good communication- Each partner should speak honestly and openly to avoid miscommunication
- Anger control- not insulting one another, not putting hands on one another, not belittling one another
- Understanding- Each partner should take time to understand what the other might be feeling

I believe this discussion is for all ages. Before you begin dating or if you've been dating for over 50 years. Abuse does not happen to only one sex or one specific age group. It can happen to anyone. My prayer for you today is that you are not ignorant to the signs of abuse or the red flags, but can recognize it to not only save yourself, but those you love from the dangers of an abusive relationship.

Merriam-Webster defines Red Flag as a warning signal.

Red flags, if not ignored, can prevent us from going through things such as heartbreak and abuse.

Often times many of us are ignorant to the red flags of emotional abuse. We believe if someone is not putting their hands on us physically we are not in an abusive relationship, but that is far from the truth.

Goodtheraphy.org defines emotional abuse as, a form of manipulation used to maintain control in a relationship. They continue to say, that this type of abuse may include verbal attacks, humiliation, intimidation, bullying, and isolation. It can cause deep emotional harm that may last for years. They define abuse as threatening behavior designed to subjugate another human being. Emotional abuse uses negative feelings like fear, guilt, and shame to control a person. Common tactics include insults, threats, coercion, and criticism. Another common technique is gaslighting, in which one person convinces the other to doubt their own memories. Emotional abuse can overlap with physical and sexual abuse, or it can appear on its own.

Red Flags
Know them, recognize them, and do not ignore them...

- Lack of communication-When an individual has a difficult time talking about their issues or expressing how they feel this can be a red flag. When it would seem most important to be open and honest, an abuser may distance themselves emotionally, leaving their partner hanging, or having to deal with a situation on their own. Whatever they are communicating is expressed through moodiness, and sometimes the "silent treatment".

I never viewed being ignored for multiple days in a row and given the silent treatment as abuse, but it is. [For instance, if a person in a relationship with you, whether intimate or not, refuses to discuss and communicate with you after a fight. But, instead a person chooses to ignore you by not responding to your phone calls, texts, or leaving the home for days or weeks, that is emotional abuse].

- Irresponsible, immature, and unpredictable behavior- Some people have trouble mastering basic life skills such as taking care of themselves, managing their finances, managing their personal space, keeping a job, and/or making plans for their life and future. As we discussed, in a previous chapter, some people are emotionally unhealthy, and they are unable to handle small crisis, resulting in them completely shutting down. If this is someone you are attempting to date or are dating, there may be little time and energy left for you and what you have going on. These people may still be growing up. In other words, it may be hard to rely on them for almost anything. They need to work on themselves, not drain you and take your focus off of what God wants you to do.

Please know that Jesus changes people, not us. The Lord may use us to help someone on their journey, but we must never forget that it is Him and Him alone that changes someone. When we remember this, we take the weight off of ourselves in attempting to be someone's "savior". Yes, we are put on this earth to reach the lost, but that does not mean entering into an intimate relationship with someone who is not walking with Christ in attempts to bring them to Him. That, my friend, is deception. You can love someone and desire for them to know Christ without compromising your relationship with Jesus.

- Lack of trust- When you observe a person not being honest with himself or herself, or other people, most likely they will not be honest with you. A person who holds himself or herself unaccountable for their actions lacks integrity and lacks respect for their partner.

Lying lips are extremely disgusting to the Lord,
But those who deal faithfully are His delight.
Proverbs 12:22 AMP

- Significant family and friends don't like your partner-
  If there is something "off" about this person that
  seems obvious to those who know you well and love
  you, you should listen to what they're telling you.
  Those on the outside of your relationship see more
  clearly than you do on the inside. I know all too well,
  of not wanting to hear it, but everyone in your life is
  not "jealous" of you, some love you and want what's
  best for you. Hear them out.

He who walks [as a companion] with wise men will be wise,
But the companions of [conceited, dull-witted] fools [are
fools themselves and] will experience harm.
Proverbs 13:20

If those around you lack wisdom as well, then they may not
see red flags and may encourage your relationship even if it
is harmful to you. Surround yourself around those with
wisdom and who have a strong relationship with Jesus

Christ. These people will be the ones to help you and keep you on the right track.

- Controlling behavior- If your significant other attempts to drive a wedge between you and other significant people in your life, this is emotional abuse. Sometimes they may be jealous of your ongoing relationships with other people in your life or they feel the need to control where you go and who you associate with. Abusive partners attempt to only allow what and who is important to them to stay in your life. Sometimes, they may make you choose them over significant others to prove you "love" them.

- A dark or secretive past. Behaviors that are suspect, illegal activities, and addictive behaviors- When these things have not been resolved and continue into your relationship, these are obvious red flags. A person who has done the necessary corrective work and continues doing so for their own good and for the good of the relationship is a different story.

- Non-resolution of past relationships-This can be their past intimate relationships or relationships with family members and friends. If a person consistently blames the other person for all of the problems that happened between them, but can't explain why the relationship is the way it is, most likely the same thing could happen with your relationship. Mature and emotionally healthy people are able to discuss past relationships and why they ended while taking some accountability.

- The person is needy. If your partner is constantly needing you to provide for them financially, spiritually, emotionally, or mentally, so much that it interferes with your ability to function, this is a red flag.

- Abusive behavior. Any form of abuse— verbal, emotional, psychological, and physical—is not just a red flag, but a huge sign telling you to get out immediately.

A red flag allows us to process what we are really feeling. Usually when we get out of difficult relationships, we say,

"He (or she) told me who he (or she) was at the very beginning, but I just didn't listen".

Please listen!

Don't ignore red flags.

For I know the thoughts I think toward you, says the Lord, thoughts of peace and not of evil, to give you a future and a hope.

Jeremiah 29:11 NKJV

Love is patient and kind. Love is not jealous or boastful or proud or rude. It does not demand its own way. It is not irritable, and it keeps no record of being wronged. It does not rejoice about injustice but rejoices whenever the truth wins out. Love never gives up, never loses faith, is always hopeful, and endures through every circumstance.

1 Corinthians 13:4-7 NLT

<u>Pray</u>

Father God, Your word says, without knowledge Your
people will perish. I thank You and praise You for wisdom
and understanding. Lord, please give me discernment to see
red flags in my life and the lives of those I love, not only in
intimate relationships, but in family and business
relationships as well. Lord, show me where I may be abusive
emotionally, verbally, and physically to those in my life and
forgive me. Help me to love the way You love and to accept
the love that You want to give. Lord, I will not settle for a
love that is not patient and kind, or a love that is jealous,
boastful, proud, or rude. Lord, I desire to love and be loved
the way you intended. I thank You for being the ultimate
example of what Love is. Make me more like You Lord by
showing me what's not like You, in me. In Jesus Name,
Amen.

I DIDN'T KNOW I WAS DEAD

CHAPTER TWELVE

SILENCE KILLS

Over the past year and a half there have been more days I've cried than days I did not. Whether it was in my car by myself on the way to work, in my bed late at night, or having an emotional outbreak in front of a loved one. I refused to seek help or really speak on it because I couldn't understand why I was feeling this way. I didn't enjoy doing the things I once did. Some days I felt as though I was this well-rounded picture taking, dance teaching, nurse and other days I was just proud of myself for showering and going to work. I tried to convince myself I'd be okay because there were people around me going through way worse things than I've ever been through. I was questioned by someone I love very much as to why I was depressed. That they know people going through real tuff times but I don't have any reason to be. I made sure I didn't speak on it again. **Words I never said.** -January 21, 2017*

Throughout this book you've seen, 'words I've never said'. These were taken from notes in my phone and on the computer, I so desperately wanted to speak about, but was too afraid to share.

In my previous relationship I never told anyone about how toxic the relationship was until I was out of it. I had to put my pride, my fear, and need to be perfect aside, speak up, and begin informing those I love about what was going on in my life. After opening my mouth, I was able to begin my

healing process. I wasn't able to be healed until I was willing.
Willing to speak up, willing to let someone else in, Jesus,
and willing to go through what I needed to go through to
heal completely.

And a woman who had [suffered from] a hemorrhage for
twelve years [and had spent all her money on physicians],
and could not be healed by anyone, came up behind Him
and touched the fringe of His outer robe, and immediately
her bleeding stopped. Jesus said, "Who touched
Me?" While they all were denying it, Peter [and those who
were with him] said, "Master, the people are crowding and
pushing against You!" But Jesus said, "Someone did touch
Me, because I was aware that power [to heal] had gone out
of Me." When the woman saw that she had not escaped
notice, she came up trembling and fell down before Him.
She declared in the presence of all the people the reason
why she had touched Him, and how she had been
immediately healed. He said to her, "Daughter, your
faith [your personal trust and confidence in Me] has made
you well. Go in peace (untroubled, undisturbed well-being)."
Luke 8:43-48 AMP

Will we have faith, to just get close enough to be touched by
Jesus, and be healed?

In photography, you can either shoot in RAW or JPEG
formatting. When you shoot in JPEG, the photos look better
at first because you allow your camera to process and edit it
for you. But when shooting in JPEG, a lot of the file's

contents are lost, so you can't make the same adjustments you can when you shoot in RAW. When you shoot in RAW, these files are uncompressed, so they come out looking flat and dark. Although, they don't look good at first, when shooting in RAW, you have complete control over the images you're editing. If I took a picture and showed everyone the photo in JPEG and RAW; they would choose the JPEG one, because it looks better. But when I sit down and try to edit that photo, I will not have complete control over it. This is because I allowed the camera to do the work for me, consequently, some of the contents of that photo got lost. Although, shooting in JPEG is easier, since the camera will do all the work for me, shooting in RAW allows me to bring the photo to its **VERY BEST IMAGE**.

I believe this is why some of us have not been healed completely. We'd rather look good quicker than going through the necessary process to become whole. We aren't opening our mouths and confessing **everything** we need, to be set free. We are allowing other things in life to speak for us; like our impressive career, nice car, beautiful family, successful business, huge following on social media, or our attractive appearance. Don't hide behind these things. Like a JPEG image allows the camera to do the work for us, we allow the things of this world do the work for us. When

136

people talked about me I was good! I graduated college with my bachelors of science and nursing at 21 years old, I had an amazing job with benefits, lived in a beautiful townhome with my best friend, owned my own business, and traveled frequently with friends. But behind all of that, I was holding onto secrets, secrets that were killing me, daily.

Therefore, confess your sins to one another [your false steps, your offenses], and pray for one another, that you may be healed and restored. The heartfelt and persistent prayer of a righteous man (believer) can accomplish much [when put into action and made effective by God—it is dynamic and can have tremendous power].

James 5:16 AMP

Too many of us are like a JPEG image and are desiring to look good immediately. We want quick and easy. But the truth is, being changed into who God wants us to be is not always easy. It takes an intentional surrender. It takes daily repentance and continual confessions.

Being a RAW image is choosing to be vulnerable. Like choosing to walk up to the altar in front of the entire congregation and confessing you have backslidden. Choosing to expose the areas that you fell into sin, to an accountability partner, so that you can receive prayer. Choosing to open up to someone you love and telling them you need help! Open up to God. Ask Jesus to come into your life and heal you. He will and He wants to!

We cannot allow our fears, shame, and pride to keep our mouths closed. The enemy is rejoicing each day you allow to pass by in silence.

What have you been holding in that's keeping you from being free?

What have you delayed being healed?

It's too heavy.

It's stopping you from living.

Confess.

It doesn't matter what people think or what people will say. Stop thinking about them right now. Think about Jesus and how He feels about you. He loves you and He will protect you. Everything the enemy has tried to use to harm you, will be used for your good in Jesus name! Everything the enemy is trying to use to stop the plan God has for your life, will be brought down right now in Jesus name. Silence kills. You will not die. You will open your mouth and be set free, in Jesus Name.

I love and value transparent people. Too often we all try to paint this pretty picture on social media that is not our complete truth. (I am guilty) We all may be going through things but it's human nature (and at times not anyone's business) to remain silent or selective about the things we share. But it's those transparent people who chose to speak up about their truth, which may deliver someone else out of theirs. My heart has been heavy and I've been beating myself up for keeping certain things to myself for so long. As I'm writing I promise to be transparent. I will not omit pieces of my truth to make someone else feel comfortable. Real isn't always pretty.
Words I never said. -February 3, 2017

Declare...
I will not die from fear to speak. Jesus is the only one with full power and authority in my life. I will speak up and I will be set free.

I will live, I will not die.

In Jesus Name, Amen.

CHAPTER THIRTEEN
HOPELESSNESS KILLS

I remember my 23rd birthday week, vividly. I remember trying to make multiple plans to celebrate and none of them ever happened. Instead, as my birthday arrived, I brought the night in with two of my close friends. At midnight they took a couple shots of Hennessy, while I took shots of water. We sat up and laughed and I shared my little secret with them.

I was pregnant.

I found out about a month before by jokingly taking a pregnancy test with a friend only for mine to come back positive. I wasn't really sure how to feel because that was not in my current life plan, so my boyfriend and I sat up all night pretty much silent.

As time went on we became more accepting of the new life we were about to enter, started thinking of names, and future plans. We began to go to my OBGYN and watched the ultrasound and saw and heard the heartbeat together. It was pretty exciting!

During the day of my birthday my parents wanted to take me out to eat. We went to Cheesecake Factory and I waited until it was time to get dessert to mumble the words, "I have something to tell you guys." My mom gave me that look like she already knew what I was going to say.

"I'm pregnant."

My mom started crying and my dad quickly embraced me with the biggest hug and told me he loved me. My mom stood behind him with tears rolling down her face and followed with another hug. I was glad I had finally told them. We were holding in that secret for over two months now. Now that my parents knew, I was really excited! Being a mother is something I've always dreamed of. I love children so much and I always knew I would be a great mother one day. I was looking forward to meeting my precious baby girl or boy. Then I began to think, I wonder if she or he would look like me?

Two days after my birthday, September 23, my boyfriend

141

and I went to my doctor's appointment. I was getting an ultrasound and all I remember is the doctor saying, "This isn't good." I look up like, "What isn't good"?! He paused and went on to say, "There's no heartbeat". My stomach dropped to my feet. Wait. No baby? But we talked about baby names, we talked about plans to move, we already told people......

In their hearts humans plan their course, but the Lord establishes their steps.
Proverbs 16:9 NIV

"I'm really sorry... It's not your fault, miscarriages are very common, they happen in about 1 in every... blah blah blah blah blah..." I heard nothing else after that.
My boyfriend and I went to the car with really nothing to say. He gave me a big hug in the parking lot, but neither one of us could articulate how we felt.

I went home that day so confused.

When we found out there would be no baby, I had to get a surgical D&C. This is a surgery to remove the parts of the baby that already began to form. Reality set in that it wasn't my time to have a child and at that moment, having another one seemed so far away and unrealistic.

If I was married I could have just tried again, but after my surgery the doctor came in the room and said so nonchalantly, I'll send birth control pills to your pharmacy!

I was thinking, who said I wanted to be on birth control? We never discussed this. But I said nothing.

I tried to look at the positives of not being pregnant anymore. I can drink alcohol again! I can eat turkey sandwiches! (I love turkey lol) I can go to Cedar Point and get on all the roller coasters... The list continued. But there was an emptiness left inside of me. There was also a bitterness I had that I never admitted. Of course, everyone and their mother became pregnant after this. I would congratulate them, but deep down in my heart I was jealous and confused. Why do they get to keep their baby, God?

I didn't want to admit it, but for months I was not only sad, but I was anxious about my future. I was fearful, bitter, and I had absolutely no desire to do the things I used to do. I was depressed. It took everything in me to go to work and take care of people, as if I didn't need to be at home taking care of myself, mentally. I was at a job I hated and I was beginning to lose grasp of the little bit of faith I had left. I didn't even want to be around babies, and I love babies!

I had been sad before, but I could not shake this sadness this time. I had no joy. I had no hope. All I knew was that I wasn't going to be a mother and life just didn't make sense anymore.

Why did I have to go through that?

I would pray about it, but then felt as though I shouldn't pray because I felt like God would be like, "well you shouldn't be out here getting pregnant anyway because you aren't married". So, I stopped praying.

How wrong I was about who God is and His character!

I also knew many other women went through miscarriages so I thought, I need to just get over it like they did...
I remember laying in my bed multiple nights thinking, what would people think if I was no longer alive? Would people really be upset?

I never thought I would be the one to consider suicide, but the thought crossed my mind multiple times. My boyfriend and I both experienced a downward spiral. A couple of months after all of this happened was when the physical abuse began.

Would things ever get better?

'For I know the plans and thoughts that I have for you,' says the Lord, 'plans for peace and well-being and not for disaster, to give you a future and a hope.

Jeremiah 29:11 AMP

CHAPTER FOURTEEN
UNFORGIVENESS KILLS

I love children because they remind us of how we all should
be. You can yell at a child, punish them, or hurt their
feelings and minutes later they are hugging you and telling
you how great you are. Yet as adults, we are constantly
reminded not to talk to someone, reciprocate how they
treated us, or cut them out of our lives due to offense.

To be completely honest, unforgiveness was not something
that I necessarily struggled with. I always thought something
was wrong with me because I forgave "too quickly". But
there's no such thing. Society tells us that, but not The
Word of God.

Colossians 3:13 says in the message bible,

*Be even-tempered, content with second place, quick to
forgive an offense. Forgive as quickly and completely as the
Master forgave you.*

My issue was that after I forgave, I would continue to allow a
person to hurt, manipulate, or deceive me. My issue was not
forgiveness, but wisdom. Forgiveness does not mean

146

allowing someone access back into our lives. Forgiveness is releasing that person to God and not holding bitterness, resentment, and ill feelings toward them.

I have forgiven someone and still blocked their number and them on social media. Blocking them did not mean I was bitter, it was me using wisdom that if someone has not changed and are harmful or toxic they must go.

When we hold onto offense, it only harms us and what God wants to do in our lives... not our offender.

If you forgive those who sin against you, your heavenly Father will forgive you. But if you refuse to forgive others, your Father will not forgive your sins.

Matthew 6:14-15 NLT

Joyce Meyer is an amazing example when it comes to forgiving others. I appreciate her transparency so much.

In her blog, 'Life Beyond Abuse', she wrote,

I was sexually, mentally, emotionally and verbally abused by my father as far back as I can remember until I left home at the age of eighteen. He did many terrible things...some which are too distasteful for me to talk about publicly. But I want to share my testimony because so many people have been hurt, and they need to realize that someone has made it through their struggles so they can have hope.

More than anything, I want you to know and really understand that anyone who has been abused can fully recover if they will give their life completely to Jesus.

What Does "Abuse" Mean?

Abuse is defined as "to be misused, used improperly or to be wasted; to use in such a way as to cause harm or damage; to be treated cruelly." Any time we are misused or used for a purpose other than what God intended, it's damaging. And I realize many people can relate to this. For some of you reading this article, I'm just telling your story. You know what it's like to live with a terrible, shameful secret that is eating you alive.

My father was a mean, controlling, and manipulative person for most of his life. He was unpredictable and unstable. As a result, the atmosphere of our home was super-charged with fear because you never knew if what you did would make him mad or not.

We always did what he wanted to do, when he wanted to do it. We watched what he wanted to watch on TV, went to bed when he went to bed, got up when he got up, and ate the meals he wanted us to eat...everything in our home was determined by his moods and what he wanted.

The sexual abuse started when I was very young, and when he decided I was mature enough, he took things even further. From this point until I was eighteen, he raped me at least once a week. My father, whom I was supposed to be able to trust and who was supposed to keep me safe, was the person I came to fear the most.

Feelings of Shame and Loneliness

148

I was so profoundly ashamed because of this. I was ashamed of me, and I was ashamed of my father and what he did. I was also constantly afraid. There was no place I ever felt safe growing up. I don't think we can even begin to imagine what kind of damage this does to a child.

At school I pretended I had a normal life, but I felt lonely all the time and different from everyone else. I never felt like I fit in, and I wasn't allowed to participate in after-school activities, go to sports events or parties or date boys. Many times I had to make up stories about why I couldn't do anything with my classmates. For so long I lived with pretense and lies.

What I learned about love was actually perversion. My father told me what he did to me was special and because he loved me. He said everything he did was good, but it had to be our secret because no one else would understand and it would cause problems in the family. It became my burden not to let my pain cause problems in our family. And as long as I kept this secret, I couldn't get free from the pain of it.

You may be wondering, Joyce, where was God in all of this? He was there. He didn't get me out of the situation when I was a child, but He did give me the strength to get through it. It's true my father abused me and didn't love and protect me the way he should have, and at times it seemed no one would ever help me and it would never end.

But God always had a plan for my life, and He has redeemed me. He has taken what Satan meant for harm and turned it into something good (see Romans 8:28). He has taken away my shame and given me a double reward and recompense (see Isaiah 6:7).

You may be thinking you would never forgive someone for doing that to you or someone you love, I thought the same thing at first. Yet, Joyce Forgave Her Father.

In her blog, From Fear to Forgiveness she wrote,

When I was about 45 years old, God gave me an undeniable urge to confront my father, who had sexually abused me throughout my childhood. I was terrified to experience his anger again, and I did. But I also accomplished what God was leading me to do. And it helped me break free. Here's what I want to help you understand: When God gives you direction for your life, don't run from it, embrace it...no matter how scary or difficult it may seem. Let God lead you step by step, believing He loves you and that He's acting on your behalf.

Joyce Meyer has always been someone I looked up to. Even when I was in the world doing my own thing I would print off her devotionals at work from her website and read them. I looked up to her so much because of her transparency and every time I read or listened to a message from her, she planted a seed in my life.

I used her particular story of forgiveness in my book because I believe some of you needed to hear it. Joyce Meyer is free to preach her testimony about her father without bitterness and ill feelings toward him because she forgave him.

150

Just as she forgave her father I had to forgive some people in my life.

If you are wondering if I forgave my ex I spoke about at the beginning of this book, absolutely! I love him and God has a purpose and plan for his life. If God needs to use me to speak to him I am more than willing. We communicate frequently now and are able to laugh about past mistakes we both made. God is so good! My ex-boyfriend was never a bad or evil person. He was hurting and consequently hurt other people. Many of you are hurting and not realizing you are hurting other people. There were times I was hurting, hurt other people, and I'm thankful that they showed me grace and mercy.

Forgiveness is not easy, but it's necessary to truly be free and do the things The Lord is calling us to do.

Why should we forgive?
1. The bible tells us to
2. If we do not forgive others, God will not forgive us
3. Unforgiveness harbors sin and sin leads to death
4. We will have peace in our mind, body, and soul

5. When we forgive others, they are experiencing
   Christ though our forgiveness

In the book The Power of Prophetic Prayer, Kynan Bridges, shared this story,

I have had my share of phenomenal encounters. Once, a woman came all the way from Mississippi to our healing school in Tampa. She was desperate to be healed. We led the entire school in prayer of release from anger and bitterness. This woman was instantly healed from fibromyalgia and chronic migraine headaches. Praise the name of Jehovah, for He is truly our Healer!

Wow. The reason she was suffering from a physical illness was because of her anger and bitterness.

Father God, help us to forgive quickly.

Pray

Father God, thank You for forgiving me of my sins and remembering them no more. Thank You for showing me the ultimate example of forgiveness by forgetting everything I've done apart from You and giving me a new life to be free to love and to pursue all that You have for me to pursue. Thank You for showing me those I need to forgive. Thank You for showing me where I need healing. Thank You for showing me where I need to be more graceful, more loving, and more kind. Thank You for giving me the revelation that people desperately need You and that they hurt me because they don't know You and don't know what they are doing. Give me the strength to forgive them. I release, (insert name), over to You right now. I pray, Lord, that they will find You. I pray that I will not harvest bitterness towards them or continue to speak wrongly about them and consequently mess up my life. I don't want to harvest bitterness and to be sick. I do not want to be sick mentally, physically, or spiritually. So right now, Lord, heal me. Heal my mind, my body, and my soul. I know that I am free to walk and do the things You have called me to do because I have forgiven (insert name). I thank You and I praise You for taking this burden from me and for fighting my battles. In Jesus Name, Amen.

CHAPTER FIFTEEN

MORE LIFE

People generally fall into one of three groups: the few who make things happen, the many who watch things happen, and the overwhelming majority who have no notion of what happens. Every person is either a creator of fact or a creature of circumstance. He either puts color into his environment, or, like a chameleon, takes color from his environment.
Dr. Myles Munroe

I got asked, after coming back home to Christ, what were my days like before coming back home to Him?

I thought about it and responded, well I would wake up and go to work, work 12 hours, come home, smoke, eat, talk and watch TV with my boyfriend, then go to bed. On my days off, I would wake up, smoke, go get something to eat, take a 3-hour nap, wake up, smoke again, see what my friends were doing, get with them, smoke, and repeat. That was pretty much my schedule. Every now and then we would switch it up a little, but that was the gist.

I was stagnant.

Merriam-Webster defines stagnant as:

1. not flowing in a current or stream
2. without inflow and outflow
3. STALE
4. not advancing or developing

We need to learn to get out of our routines from time to time.

How are we going to welcome miracles if we are stuck doing the same thing, the same way, every single day of our lives? Now if you're thinking, but I love routine, I agree, I do too. I want my cup of coffee in the morning and I want my time by myself of quietness. When my coworker begins talking at what seems like 500 words per minute at 8am, I'm like REALLY?

Side Note: I need y'all to begin praying for me NOW for when it's my time to be married and have children. I love being by myself a little too much! Lol.

Anywho, one weekend in February of 2019 The Lord shook up my routine a little bit. I had a 30-minute photoshoot scheduled on a Friday night that was originally at 8pm. I normally do not schedule photoshoots that late, but agreed to photograph a birthday shoot at that time. I was contacted by a young man who was purchasing a shoot for his girlfriend's 18th birthday. A couple of days before the photoshoot he asked if he could change the time to 8:30pm. Then the day of the shoot, he asked a couple of hours before 8:30 pm if he could change the time to 9pm. At this point I was slightly annoyed that he kept rescheduling the time. Not only was it a Friday night, but I had my brother coming with me to assist with carrying the studio equipment and set up lighting. Nevertheless, I agreed to the changes.

The morning of this shoot I was reading out of my book, The Power of Prophetic Prayer by Kynan Bridges. In the book that day the prayer was,

Someone is going to favor you financially today...

As my brother and I arrived at the Airbnb where the shoot was taking place, the man who I was in contact with was not there yet, but sent his girlfriend out to get us. It was a little before 9pm and the birthday girl and her friends were still not ready. The boyfriend arrived around 9:20pm and stated however much time they ended up going over he would pay for it. As my brother and I sat waiting, it wasn't until about

9:40pm that they were ready to begin taking photos. Now, I mentioned before that he originally only scheduled a 30-minute shoot. So, by 9:40 we should have already been out the door, but we did not end up leaving until after 11pm.

The 30-minute studio shoot was only $200. Including travel and late fees, that 30-minute $200 studio photoshoot turned into a 2-hour $600 studio photoshoot. When the shoot was over, I informed him of the cost and the young man so nicely pulled $400 out of his pocket and handed it to me after already paying the original balance of $160 online. He thanked my brother and I so much for coming to them, being so flexible, and being so patient. I literally was mind blown that what I prayed about, being favored financially, came true. I just had to get out of my routine and take off the parameters of who I believed my blessing would come through. I gave $200 to my brother for assisting me and went home and gave the other $200 to my mother because I owed her money.

Thank you, Jesus.

The next day was Saturday and I had to dance spontaneously at church that evening. I normally do not attend Saturday evening service, but that Sunday I had a bridal expo to attend with my brother for our wedding photography company, Your Wedding Creatives. The event was from 10am-2pm, so I was going to miss 11am service.

Minister Daphne Harris spoke the word that evening and when she was done she came off the platform and said, "I have two prophetic words for two people in here today". Instantly I thought "she's going to call me out". I was right. After speaking to the first person she subtly walked over to me and said, Olivia raise your hand. *Raised hand* She said Olivia is a registered nurse and she helps people get well at her job. Am I right? I shook my head yes. Well, she continued to say, The Lord has given you the gift of healing. You will be able to lay hands on the sick and they will recover, you will be able to lay hands on the broken hearted and they will be healed, and you will be able to lay hands on the captives and they will be set free. And the Lord is saying this is not a word for you to walk in 10 years from now, but this word is for you to walk in right now.

My God!

Shortly after this, Ms. Beverly Moore signaled for me to come over and talk to her. She was the host of the evening. She whispered, "I believe you already knew that". I did but had been waiting on another confirmation. She continued to say, "I'm going to call some people up here who need healing and you're going to pray for them. I will be standing right beside you and you don't need to be afraid"! *Gulp* And that is exactly what happened! She asked those who needed healing to come forth and about 15 people came forward. I prayed in the Holy Spirit and began to go down the line one by one and pray.

My God!

When I was finished, all I could do was weep and praise God. Each person I prayed for told me everything I had prayed was exactly what they needed to hear and that they instantly felt better.

Glory be to God because I didn't even know their names!

It was another divine encounter that I had to get out of my routine to experience.

The next day, on Sunday, was the Bridal Expo. Our table was set up right in the front and in the next room was another photography company. That particular photography business had been in business for over 35 years, longer than both my brother and I had been living. When the expo was over my brother went over to talk to the owner and I followed shortly after. The owner began to explain to us that he made 8.5 million dollars from photography last year.

Yes.

8.5 million dollars...

As he continued telling us his story he began to drop tip after tip, and gem after gem. He informed us where he got his books, banners, and prints. He gave us insight on how to maximize our money, how to advertise efficiently, and was not selfish at all by holding back any knowledge he had. It was a great conversation and extremely inspirational. This final divine encounter ended my weekend with a bang.

Will you believe me when I say The Lord wants to expand us, but we have to first be willing to get out of the same routine?

Leaders prepare while other people play. Leaders understand planned neglect. Neglecting temporary pleasure for long-term gain is a principle of preparation. While others are having fun, you must stay focused on your long-term goal. Your preparation may be private for your public performance. Valuing solitude while you're out of the public eye is critical. My model for leadership, Jesus, would withdraw himself to the wilderness, desert, and quiet places for prayer and meditation. Valuing times of solitude is where we learn to hear His voice.
Bishop LaFayette Scales

Maybe your routine right now is doing a bunch of different things and The Lord is calling you to switch it up and be alone. Obey. As Bishop LaFayette Scales said, "Neglecting temporary pleasure for long-term gain is a principle of preparation".

If the Lord is calling you to be alone in this season, He is preparing you. Don't delay what he has for you.

Ask yourself...
Am I currently connected to Christ?
Am I communicating with Him daily and allowing Him to impart His word in me?
Am I imparting what He gave me to others?
Are my fruits visible?
Am I maturing and developing?

Am I being obedient to what The Lord is asking me to do in this season?

Do I know what The Lord wants me to do in this season?

If you answered no to any of these questions, that's okay! I'm glad you're here! Sometimes we allow the cares and worries of life to slow us down and get us off track. Get back on track today!

Pray

Father God, I thank You and praise You for giving me life. I want to live life abundantly, the way that You planned for me to live from the beginning. Father God, forgive me for being stagnant. Forgive me for not breaking up my routine and for being afraid to move when You say move. Forgive me for not breaking up my routine and being afraid to sit when You say sit. Lord, I desire to be on the same page as You. Lord, I thank You for divine encounters in my life. I thank You for miracles in my life. I thank You for imparting Your blessings and favor on me everywhere I go. In Jesus Name, Amen.

I DIDN'T KNOW I WAS DEAD

CHAPTER SIXTEEN

WHEN DID WE STOP DREAMING?

You are a dreamer, I put that in you. You have passion, I put that there too. I watch you wonder what's next as you cringe at that desk. No this is not it, please do not quit. Please trust in My time, because I trust you, which is why I laid this straight path in front of you. Follow it. My promises were not made in vain. We have a covenant, so no need to worry, just call upon My name. Keep planting those seeds and don't lose hope in your dream. Beloved, you will not lose for you are on My team.

That's the real trouble with the world, too many people grow up. They forget...
Walt Disney

I took a trip to Walt Disney world in 2018 with my family. I went on multiple vacations that year, but Disney was my absolute favorite. I'm the biggest kid and am unashamed about it! I was more excited to see the characters crossing the street than my nine-year-old niece.

We watched the light show at Magic Kingdom at the end of one night and this is how it began...

Each of us have a dream. A heart's desire. It calls to us. And when we are brave enough to listen and bold enough to pursue, that dream will lead us on a journey to discover who

*we are meant to be. All we have to do is look inside our
hearts and unlock the magic within.*

Disney. Is. So. Deep!

It spoke right to me! I was like, Jesus?

The entire time I was walking around the park, all I could
think about was how much creativity was put into making the
park the experience that it was. People are getting paid to
create and to do what they love to do! That thought stirred
me up so much. People are working their dream job, yet I
was working at a job living paycheck to paycheck doing
something that was not fueling my creativity at all.

When did I stop dreaming?

Ever since I was a little girl I have been dramatic, creative,
and had quite the imagination. A friend of mine, Chelsea
would always say in nursing school we pictured life as a
musical!

Our imaginations would randomly drift away from "real life"
and we would picture everyone breaking out in dance and
song. Lol

That's kind of how I see life now. You may catch me chuckling to myself because of something I imagined in my head. If I spoke it, it would sound crazy so the thought is usually just for my own entertainment. I believe each of us has something we have dreamed about whether it's once, or twice, or a continual thing.

I dream about what it will be like being married one day and have a family. I smile when I think about it because I'll have more of an excuse to watch all of the childish movies I love to watch.

I dream about having my own photography studio. I dream about what it will look like, what it will smell like, and what music will set the atmosphere.

I dream about what my boutique will be like. I dream about the divine encounters that will take place in this shop. How people will come in shopping for clothes and leave with an encounter from Jesus.

I dream about how this book will be in the hands of many. I dream about someone being excited to grab a cup of coffee and sit in their bed to just dive in. I dream about how their life will be changed for the better.

Yup, I've dreamed about you!

I dream about all of my family and friends walking with Christ and being purposeful in everything they do. I dream about them seeing their dreams come true.

All of these dreams and visions make me happy. They make me even more happy because I believe they will come true.

I teach dance and one of our starlights, who was about four years old at the time, looked inside the fake pond we made with eyes super wide and bright. She smiled and said, I see a mermaid in there! I looked down and of course didn't see a mermaid, but I responded, "Wow yes, she's beautiful"!

I refused to discredit this four-year old's imagination and what she believed was in there.

It's not about what we see but what we believe!

That little girl believed a mermaid was in that pond. She didn't see one, but she believed it was there.

For we live by believing and not by seeing.
2 Corinthians 5:7 NLT

This is why we aren't supposed to tell everyone our dreams because everyone is not going to be able to see our dreams the way we do. The Lord gave you the vision, so stop getting frustrated when other people aren't as excited as you.

The key to dreaming is believing.

Be bold enough to pursue your dreams. If those dreams and desires align with God's will and purpose for your life, He will give them to you, if you do the work!

Take delight in the LORD, and he will give you your heart's desires.
Psalm 37:4 NLT

And as you dream... pray for patience.

Understand that your dreams and your discomfort go hand in hand. You dream about how things could be so you are uncomfortable with how they are presently.
Social Club Misfits

As you continue to dream, ask the Lord for patience. Trust in His timing because He's in no hurry. Enjoy each season and each stage. Don't reject small beginnings, but rejoice as you learn, mature, and grow.

By their nature, big dreams don't seem realistic at all!
Sam Chand

Do you believe your dreams can come true?

CHAPTER SEVENTEEN

WHEN DID WE STOP BELIEVING?

Great moves of God are usually preceded by simple acts of obedience.
Steven Furtick

But Samuel replied,

What is more pleasing to the Lord:
your burnt offerings and sacrifices
or your obedience to his voice?
Listen! Obedience is better than sacrifice,
and submission is better than offering the fat of rams.

1 Samuel 15:22 NLT

Obedience is defined as compliance with an order, request, or law or submission to another's authority.

Sacrifice is defined as an act of giving up something valued for the sake of something else regarded as more important or worthy.

The Lord gave me the vision for my online boutique, Can We Live, at the beginning of 2018. When I was starting my online boutique, I had absolutely no idea what I was doing or what I was getting myself into. I knew the Lord was calling me to start it as well as write this book, but I was super unsure about it because it was an unfamiliar territory. I had been successful in running my photography business for two years, but retail was a new ball game.

Yet, I knew The Lord wanted me to start it at the time I did.

When I went to Cheryl Singletary's women's conference in May, in Atlanta, Georgia called, I Still Have Oil, one of the prophets spoke to me and said,

I hear The Lord saying He is giving you a blank check right now... because you have been faithful over little He can trust you over much. I hear him asking you, daughter what is it that you want from me? Because I'm giving you a blank check. He wants you to Respond BIG, don't think little but think BIG. Speak out what you really want. Speak out what's really on your heart. Speak out that business that you want because He said He'll give it to you. Even the know how, the I don't know how to run a business? Well that's okay because I'm The Lord and I can show you how to run a successful business. I can teach you how to run a successful business because you're teachable. Because you're obedient. So that idea that you think is little, that no one is really listening to right now, that business idea, you better start writing a business plan, not just the idea, write a business plan, write it out on paper. The Lord says write the vision and make it plain. With your vision you need to set due dates because there are things that are going to start lining up for you because God says I can trust you and I know that what I give to you you're going to give back to my people. And because He can trust you the windows of heaven over your life remain open. There's some that come and try to shut it. There's some that come and try to steal it but He said "no", know what I do no one can undo. What I say no one can undo.

Jesus!

I still get chills listening to this and all of the prophecies I have recorded.

I was obedient to the voice of The Lord and started a business plan. I went to the secretary of state and registered CAN WE LIVE as an LLC and I obtained my vendor's license to sell clothes. I set the date for the launch for September 22, 2018, the first day of fall. I set my only free weekend it seemed like, to go back to Atlanta, to their buyer's mart, at the end of July to search for clothes to put into my boutique. I had all of these dates in my planner, yet I was still feeling way over my head.

When the weekend came to go down to Atlanta, to shop, I brought two empty suitcases because I was believing The Lord for merchandise to bring home. I didn't know from what store, but I was believing I would have something! My dad and my nephew accompanied me to Atlanta's America's Mart and we started the search for some apparel. The first store I went in everything was way too expensive. The price tags ranged from $80-$150 and if I had to buy them at that price that meant I had to sell the clothes for at least $160-$300 to make a profit. I knew I was in the wrong store for my target audience, so I continued on. The next couple of stores I walked in the associates there barely paid me any attention. They didn't even get up from their computers to come and speak to me, but instead looked at me like, "she's not going to buy anything". Nevertheless, I still asked questions, but knew those stores weren't it either. Then I went into an open store that I loved! I began to gather clothes in my hand until an associate came in and said, "Ma'am sorry we're closed because we are getting ready for our show" ... "Oh, I replied, the door was open..." "That's only because we are moving things in and out, but we aren't selling anything today, but here's our card". So, I put the clothes down and walked out.

At this point I was extremely frustrated and over it thinking, why did I decide to do this again?

I went down one floor and walked around the corner to see this store lit up and, I kid you not, a heavenly sound came from it. I walked in to have this bright and bubbly girl approach me and say can I help you? I just started smiling because it was like an AHHHH moment. I told her that I was starting an online boutique and needed clothes and she began to help me right away. She asked me where the name Can We Live came from and I told her it was based off of a book I was writing, I Didn't Know I Was Dead.

The name of the company was called Before You and I asked her where it originated ...

She said,

"Well the owners dad is a pastor and it came from a verse in the bible..."

*The LORD himself goes **before you** and will be with you; he will never leave you nor forsake you. Do not be afraid; do not be discouraged.*

Deuteronomy 31:8 NIV

Thank you, Lord.

***Before** I formed **you** in the womb I knew you, **before you** were born I set you apart; I appointed you as a prophet to the nations.*

Jeremiah 1:5 NIV

You're faithful Lord.

I ended up leaving that day with my two suitcases full! All the Lord asked of me was to be obedient and go, even though I didn't know what was waiting for me!

When I got back home I began to plan more for the launch. Website building, photoshoots, and unfun necessary legal tasks. Money began to get tighter and tighter, and credit card debt got bigger and bigger. I reached out to an accountant because I knew I needed her help! After she informed me of her monthly pricing I was like ehhh okay I'll get back with you! She ended up e-mailing and telling me she'll give me a free in person 1-hour consultation. During this "consultation" she made me a QuickBooks account and hooked it up to my Shopify website so it would automatically track my taxes for me.

Words could not express the gratefulness I had for the favor she showed me that day!

But my God shall supply all your need according to his riches in glory by Christ Jesus.
Philippians 4:19 KJV

Still broke and still preparing for the launch, I was spending a lot of time with my friend, who also happened to be one of Can We Live's models, Samara. We had dinner at a vegan burger spot in downtown Columbus and just chatted. After dinner she said, I want to give you something. She handed me a little gold card and I was like what's this? She worked at Chipotle's corporate office and told me she got a chipotle card with money loaded on it each month and HANDED IT TO ME.
Pause.

I DIDN'T KNOW I WAS DEAD

Just wait one second.

Anyone who knows me, knows I LOVE chipotle and will eat chipotle every single day. Okay? Every. Single. Day.

When I tell you during this time I barely had money to buy food, and this girl just handed me a chipotle gift card. Not just any gift card, but to my favorite place?

If I didn't believe in God before, this was the moment I would have!

That is why I tell you not to worry about everyday life—whether you have enough food and drink, or enough clothes to wear. Isn't life more than food, and your body more than clothing? Look at the birds. They don't plant or harvest or store food in barns, for your heavenly Father feeds them. And aren't you far more valuable to him than they are? Can all your worries add a single moment to your life? "And why worry about your clothing? Look at the lilies of the field and how they grow. They don't work or make their clothing, yet Solomon in all his glory was not dressed as beautifully as they are. And if God cares so wonderfully for wildflowers that are here today and thrown into the fire tomorrow, he will certainly care for you. Why do you have so little faith? "So don't worry about these things, saying, 'What will we eat? What will we drink? What will we wear?' These things dominate the thoughts of unbelievers, but your heavenly Father already knows all your needs. Seek the Kingdom of God above all else, and live righteously, and he will give you everything you need. "So don't worry about tomorrow, for tomorrow will bring its own worries. Today's trouble is enough for today.

Matthew 6:25-34 NLT

The Lord never called for me to worry, He called for me to TRUST HIM and He would supply my every need. The Lord did not necessarily give me money in the form of dollars to provide for me during this time, but He gave me everything that I needed.

Stop waiting for what you want and start working what you have. This can turn your great frustration into your greatest potential innovation. If you'll do your part, God will begin to do what only He can do: He'll make your box bigger.

Steven Furtick

Are you having trouble believing?

A lot of us believe in God, yet do not believe in what He can and WILL do.

Repent and say this prayer with me...

Lord, please forgive me for being disobedient. Lord, I thank You for wanting to supply all of my needs. I thank You for always taking care of me and providing for me and for my family. Lord, increase my faith. Your word says, without faith it is impossible to please You. Show me where I lack faith and teach me to live a life that is pleasing to You. I love You Lord. In Jesus Name, Amen.

CHAPTER EIGHTEEN

FEAR KILLS

My dearest daughter,
Today is your sixteenth birthday. Congratulations. I present
you with this diary, to fill the pages with your special
thoughts - special thoughts of your wonderful life.
It is a custom in my family to pass on a piece of wisdom
when one reaches this age. I pass it on to you, as my father
passed it on to me.

Amelia, courage is not the absence of fear, but rather the
judgement that something else is more important than fear.
The brave may not live forever, but the cautious do not live
at all.

From now on, you'll be traveling the road between who you
think you are and who you can be. The key is to allow
yourself to make the journey.

I also want you to know: I loved your mother very much and
still think of her often.
Happy birthday, my Mia.
All my love,
Your father

"The brave will not live forever, but the cautious will not live
at all." Tears were streaming down my face as if that was the
first time I saw the movie Princess Diaries. Yet, at 26 I re-
watch movies with new insight and revelation hearing from
God, once again, through Disney.

What things am I afraid?

I'm afraid of failing.

I'm afraid of not doing what I'm supposed to be doing.

I'm afraid of letting someone down.

I'm afraid of being wrong.

I'm afraid of offending someone.

I'm afraid of not knowing.

I'm afraid of people finding out the real me is this extremely flawed, overly sensitive, spoiled brat who has a big heart yet has many areas to grow.

Courage is not the absence of fear, but rather the judgement that something else is more important than fear.

Something else is more important than fear...

Or how about someone else...

Because one person disobeyed God, many became sinners. But because one other person obeyed God, many will be made righteous.
Romans 5:19 NLT

Fear is a distraction.

Fear distracts us from doing what The Lord is calling us to do. When we are disobedient to God, it not only affects us but effects so many others who are connected to our purpose.

Our fears effect more than just you and me, which should be even more of a sense of urgency to break free!

Such love has no fear, because perfect love expels all fear. If we are afraid, it is for fear of punishment, and this shows that we have not fully experienced his perfect love.

1 John 4:18 NLT

When I first began writing and released my blog 'Love Doesn't Hurt', fear was overcome by the overflowing love of my heavenly father. I wasn't concerned about what people thought about me putting "my" business out there. I just wanted others to gain access to the freedom I had found. I wanted everyone to encounter Jesus the way I had. I would boldly speak out and I would be quick to pray and encourage someone. Not because I was super confident in myself, but because I was on fire for Christ and confident in Him.

We now have this light shining in our hearts, but we ourselves are like fragile clay jars containing this great treasure. This makes it clear that our great power is from God, not from ourselves.
2 Corinthians 4:7

I DIDN'T KNOW I WAS DEAD

Every time I'm too afraid to take action, I realize I'm not close enough to God.

Our dreams should frighten us because they are bigger than ourselves; but they should frighten us right into the arms of our Heavenly Father! We know without Him it would be impossible!

After I went to the conference in Atlanta, I was called out by a prophet whom I had never met in my life. I was dancing and praising God and Prophet Carla Clark stopped me from dancing and laid her hand on my head while the other ministers laid hands on me as well. Prophet Carla Clark said, "The spirit of prophecy is given to you by the laying on of hands" and immediately I felt an impartation from The Holy Spirit and began weeping. I was having another divine encounter. They continued praying while I continued sobbing! My eyes were closed, but when I opened them there was a circle of people surrounding me. Everyone in my generation at that conference was on their knees with their hands stretched toward me, praying for me. It was such a powerful thing to witness! I quickly closed by eyes again because I couldn't believe what was happening.

When I left the conference Prophet Carla Clark followed up with me and said,

Hello Olivia, this is somewhat of an explanation to this weekend. I added Cheryl so that she could bear witness of the word and give oversight to the years to come. Some of this is for now. Some for your future... 1 Tim 4:12-17 Let no one despise your youth, but be an example to the believers in word, in conduct, in love, in spirit, in faith, in purity. Till I come, give attention to reading, to exhortation, to doctrine. Do not neglect the gift that is in you, which was given to you by prophecy with the laying on of the hands of the eldership. Meditate on these things; give yourself entirely to them, that your progress may be evident to all. Take heed to yourself and to the doctrine. Continue in them, for in doing this you will save both yourself and those who hear you. An anointing oil was released in your life because this weekend, I the Lord, am calling you to be a catalyst in your generation. In the coming days unlikely opportunities will arise for you to declare the word of the Lord. Trust the Holy Spirit in you. The Lord has called you to the kingdom for such a time as this. Be of good courage and don't be afraid. I would encourage you to read Jeremiah 1-3. You are called of the Lord. Get ready!!!! Pour your oil.

I had already been prophesying over people's lives, but did not realize that's what I was doing. I was just being obedient when The Lord told me to deliver a message to someone. After coming back home from this conference and realizing I had this gift, I was terrified out of my mind. So terrified that I allowed the enemy to shut my lips. I didn't want to speak, I did not want to pray, I did not want to write, and I did not want to dance.

I was being oppressed by the enemy!

I didn't realize how distracted I had become by this fear.

I don't know about you but I believed prophecies normally excited people, but for me they scared me immensely.

Lord, I don't want to mess this up!!!

It's not that I stopped believing in God, I didn't believe in me! I was scared that what The Lord was trying to do through me could not be done because I was not capable.

You have the wrong one Lord, is what I thought again and again. I didn't want to prophecy over anyone's life and be wrong! My fear was in my ability. When the Lord doesn't ask us to trust in our own abilities, but in Him.

Each time he said, "My grace is all you need. My power works best in weakness." So now I am glad to boast about my weaknesses, so that the power of Christ can work through me.

2 Corinthians 12:9 NLT

I had to realize me overcoming my fears was not just about me, but about the young girls, young boys, women, men, and elderly who are connected to my calling. They need to know that no, we may not be able to, but God IS able and we are fighting a battle that has already been won.

My prayer for you today is that you no longer allow fear to stop the word spoken over your life, before you were born, to be fulfilled. Those prophecies you rejected because you thought, "they have the wrong one" ... go back and listen to them...

God is able to do infinitely more than what we might ask or think.

<u>Pray</u>

Father Your word says perfect love casts out all fear. Lord, I do not want to go through life fearing what's next. I don't want to be anxious and I do not want to worry. Lord, my fear has been keeping me stagnant and has kept me from living. I don't want to live this way. Lord, I release all of my fears and worries unto You. I thank You for taking them and for giving me Your perfect peace. Your word says, I can do all things through You who gives me strength (Philippians 4:13) Thank You for strengthening me to do all that I am purposed to do. I will live, I will not die, and declare the works of The Lord. In Jesus Name, Amen.

CHAPTER NINETEEN

COMPARISON KILLS

There's nothing like walking in your lane and doing what
God has specifically called you to do. You NEVER have to
reinvent the wheel when the Lord will pave an entire NEW
lane for YOU.
Heather Lindsey

I can almost bet half of you unconsciously compared your
walk with mine as you read throughout this book; which is
why I chose to leave this chapter for the end. I want you to
finish this book feeling uplifted and alive, not discouraged
because you think you aren't doing enough.

But first, let me begin with saying some comparison is good.
Yup, we need others around us who are doing what they are
supposed to do to motivate us to do what we are supposed
to be doing!

But as for you, teach the things which are in agreement with
sound doctrine [which produces men and women of good
character whose lifestyle identifies them as true
Christians]. Older men are to be temperate, dignified,
sensible, sound in faith, in love, in steadfastness [Christ-like
in character]. Older women similarly are to be reverent in
their behavior, not malicious gossips nor addicted to much
wine, teaching what is right and good, so that they may
encourage the young women to tenderly love their husbands

*and their children, to be sensible, pure, makers of a home
[where God is honored], good-natured, being subject to their
own husbands, so that the word of God will not be
dishonored. In a similar way urge the young men to be
sensible and self-controlled and to behave wisely [taking life
seriously]. And in all things show yourself to be an example
of good works, with purity in doctrine [having the strictest
regard for integrity and truth], dignified, sound and beyond
reproach in instruction, so that the opponent [of the faith]
will be shamed, having nothing bad to say about us. Urge
bond-servants to be subject to their own masters in
everything, to be pleasing and not talk back, not stealing
[things, regardless of value], but proving themselves
trustworthy, so that in every respect they will adorn and do
credit to the teaching of God our Savior. For the
[remarkable, undeserved] grace of God that brings salvation
has appeared to all men. It teaches us to reject ungodliness
and worldly (immoral) desires, and to live sensible, upright,
and godly lives [lives with a purpose that reflect spiritual
maturity] in this present age, awaiting and confidently
expecting the [fulfillment of our] blessed hope and the
glorious appearing of our great God and Savior, Christ
Jesus, who [willingly] gave Himself [to be crucified] on our
behalf to redeem us and purchase our freedom from all
wickedness, and to purify for Himself a chosen and very
special people to be His own possession, who are
enthusiastic for doing what is good. Tell them these things.
Encourage and rebuke with full authority. Let no one
disregard or despise you [conduct yourself and your teaching
so as to command respect].*

Titus 2 AMP

We are supposed to be examples ourselves and we should
have Godly examples to look up to around us. Merriam-

Webster defines an example as, one that serves as a pattern
to be imitated or not to be imitated. If someone is
attempting to imitate (follow as a pattern, model, or
example) you, they will be comparing (examine the character
or qualities to discover resemblances or differences)
themselves to you.

*Therefore be imitators of God [copy Him and follow His
example], as well-beloved children [imitate their father].*
Ephesians 5:5 AMPC

This is why it is so important that we imitate God, just as
Jesus did.

Jesus talking in John 14:31 AMP says,
*but so that the world may know [without any doubt] that I
love the Father, I do exactly as the Father has commanded
Me [and act in full agreement with Him]. Get up, let us go
from here.*

People will, and should, encounter Christ through us. With
this knowledge I know I need to be obedient to what The
Lord asks of me, because other lives depend on it.

I compare, in a healthy way, areas I need to work on with those I may admire. For example, at my job, there is a nurse practitioner, Sheena, who has the patience of Jesus! Seriously, she's so patient it's annoying. Hospitals and doctor's offices can be extremely stressful and it is so easy to become overwhelmed. I've always been one to carry my emotions on my sleeves so people can easily see how I'm feeling. But, The Lord was showing me that being all over the place with my emotions is a sign of immaturity. There had been a lot of changes in our clinic within the past four years of me working there and our specific clinic always got the short end of the stick. I was over it! I would watch Sheena get mistreated by other providers and administration and she would remain peaceful, full of joy, and still do the right thing. I was ready for petty revenge! Yet, she would go over and beyond even when she didn't have to and was very consistent in her work ethic. I knew The Lord had me working with her because there were things I needed to learn and fix within myself. He was showing me Him through her.

The Lord will do that, show us Him through other people.

This is why I say some comparison is good, when it brings correction and life.

Comparison is not good when it brings condemnation and death.

If I was looking at Sheena thinking, "I really suck" or "I shouldn't even be working here because I'm not good enough", "I can't measure up". This is when comparison becomes unhealthy.

John Piper said, we can tell this is happening in us when we look at others and don't see the grace of God, but reflections of our own inferiority. We don't see them as windows into God's glory, but as mirrors into which we are asking, "Who's the fairest one of all?" — and we know it's not us. God does not place people in our lives to make us look at ourselves like wow I'm really not that amazing! No, he places people in our lives to fellowship with, learn from, love on, and grow with! He gives us people who will push us further into who He has called us to be. Don't allow comparing yourself to others lead you into jealously and selfishness. You may end up missing some of your biggest blessings and seasons of growth allowing your flesh to rule over you. What God has for you is for you, and when we fully grasp this, then we are able to fix each other's crowns and cheer one another on joyfully! There's no need to compete or compare. We don't have the same assignment!

Each and every one of us was put on this earth for a specific God-given a purpose. A purpose only we can do! Just as no one has the same DNA, none of us were put on this earth to do exactly what someone else was put on this earth to do. Though our purposes may look and sound similar, we each have our own specific one(s). This is why we are all different.

That is why some of us are small and some of us are big. Why some of us are quiet and some of us are loud. Some of us are patient and some of us are quicker and straight to the point. We have different assignments in life. Those who are quiet will be able to get into rooms the loud one can't and those of us who are loud will be able to get the attention of someone the quiet one can't.
Bishop LaFayette Scales

We need to be aware that there are things we may need to change in order to mature into the man or woman God is calling us to be, while also continuing to love who we are and recognizing God made us a certain way for a reason. I used the example of needing to be more patient and not showing my emotions on my sleeves. I know that being transparent and overly sensitive is the way God made me because I am transparent and sensitive for my purpose. My transparency is used to connect with others and bring them to Christ. My sensitivity is used to be able to feel things and see things other people may not, in order to bring others to Christ. I hated how sensitive I was and how I saw things in people others didn't, until the Lord showed me it is not just a gift, but who I am! Just as I'm quicker and straight to the point for a reason. I have zero time for nonsense, I'd rather not spend an evening complaining and gossiping or entertaining foolishness when The Lord gave me a book to write. The Lord made me this way so I could get things done, and help others get things done too!

Don't hate the way The Lord made you and do not compare yourself in an unhealthy way to how He made someone else! Your assignments are not the same!

Don't compare yourself in an unhealthy way to how you used to be either!

One of the Enemy's most effective strategies is to get you to focus on what you don't have, what you used to have, or what someone else has that you wish you had. He does this to keep you from looking around and asking, "God, what can You do through what I have?"
Steven Furtick

During a specific "quiet" season in my life I was comparing myself to how I was in previous seasons. The Lord said, Olivia, stop doing that. In multiple seasons, The Lord had me hidden to finish some things such as this book and to make straight everything that wasn't including my finances, my businesses, and my spirituality. He was preparing me for future seasons. During one particular season, I felt bad for not being as outgoing as I had been and putting on events like I was in other seasons. I felt like I wasn't being there for other people as I should, but that wasn't true. I was not publicly out there because The Lord did not want me to be. I believed my businesses weren't going to do as well because I wasn't super present on social media or that people would stop liking me because I wasn't all over their social media pages hyping them up, but that wasn't true either. The Lord needed me to trust Him and understand that in specific seasons He requires us to do specific things. If it is your time to go out and be involved, do that. But if it is your time to sit down and work on what He tells you to work on, then sit down.

This is how the enemy can easily deceive us to begin to do what we aren't supposed to be doing. You may see someone at your church starting a new series of classes over brunch every Saturday while you were instructed to fast, pray, and write your book. You are watching everyone talk about how amazing they are and how dope they are for starting this new brunch series and you feel lonely by yourself. What if I told you The Lord never told sister or brother so and so to do that brunch series? What if they did that on their own for their own glory or fame? Now you are comparing yourself to their disobedience and their distraction! We do not always know what other people are supposed to be doing in their walk with Christ, which is another reason we need to just focus on our walk!

The Lord says, you are comparing yourself to other people when they aren't even doing what I'm asking them to do. You are maturing while producing the fruit of longsuffering, upset that others around you aren't suffering, but they aren't suffering because they are avoiding what I have asked them to do in order to grow. **Stay the course.**

Pay careful attention to your own work, for then you will get the satisfaction of a job well done, and you won't need to compare yourself to anyone else.
Galatians 6:4 NLT

So then, my dear ones, just as you have always obeyed [my instructions with enthusiasm], not only in my presence, but now much more in my absence, continue to work out your salvation [that is, cultivate it, bring it to full effect, actively pursue spiritual maturity] with awe-inspired fear and trembling [using serious caution and critical self-evaluation to avoid anything that might offend God or discredit the name of Christ].

Philippians 2:12 AMP

CHAPTER TWENTY
I WILL LIVE, I WILL NOT DIE

You must decide if you are going to rob the world or bless it with the rich, valuable, potent, untapped resources locked within you.
Dr. Myles Munroe

What a journey this has been! Thank you for staying and reading! My prayer is that you have a renewed mind in regards to what living truly means. I've heard, and I'm sure you have as well, plenty of times someone say, "The devil tried to kill me". My mind always goes to someone almost getting hit by a car, getting diagnosed with cancer, or attempting to kill themselves. I pray your mind is renewed now to know that the enemy attempts to kill us in many different ways than just physically. As we have discussed, he will attempt to kill you by confusion, busyness, ignorance, fear, social media, people pleasing, perfectionism, silence, unforgiveness, and comparison. Just as God has a plan for our lives we must know and recognize that the enemy does too, and it may attack you in a way you don't realize is an attack. If you're a busy body or ambitious like myself, understand that the enemy will try to distract you from doing what you are purposed to do by things that may be good, but not God.

So how do you know if you're hearing from God?

Take away the distractions. Spend time with Him. Read His word.

What are distractions?

Everything we discussed in this book!

Social media is a distraction.

Being busy is a distraction

Trying to please people is a distraction.

Comparing yourself to others is a distraction.

Holding on to unforgiveness is a distraction.

Attempting to be perfect is a distraction.

One of my daily prayers is, Lord, there's so many things to do and so many choices to make, I just want to make the best choices today. Help me and show me what choices I need to make to stay on the right path.

I'm always getting pulled in so many different directions and never wanting to let others down. But the reality is, at times, people will be let down by my choices. It's inevitable. I can't do everything, but I can do what I'm called to do.

You can't do everything, but you can do what you are called to do!

As you were reading through this book The Lord began to reveal to you some things to begin working on, to stop working on, to do, and to stop doing. You probably have already started making the necessary changes and I am so happy for you. The enemy will attempt to distract you and to make you second guess what The Lord is telling you to do, which is why you must stay connected with Christ through prayer and His word.

I myself have all too often slipped back into my busyness and not prayed as I should or read His word as I should and found myself overwhelmed, exhausted, and anxious about everything that's on my plate. I'm not meant to do everything The Lord is calling me to do a part from Him. I can't. Which is why I literally go crazy when the first thing I take off of my full schedule, is time with Him. Let's be honest!

If you take anything away from this book, I pray you take away how vitally important it is to be connected and have a relationship with Jesus Christ. Everything else He decides to bless us with is amazing, but I am a witness that those blessings can quickly turn into burdens when we take our eyes and minds off Him.

I pray you go after your dreams, but when God begins to bless you abundantly as He will, don't forget Him!

I didn't know I was dead. I believed I was truly living and doing what I was supposed to be doing, but I wasn't. It wasn't until I got connected with Christ that all of what I spoke about in this book was revealed to me.

There's so much He wants to tell you about your life and what He wants to do through you, but you have to listen. I pray you do listen. Be okay with being set apart. Your friends and family may not be ready to turn over a new leaf with you and that's okay. The alone time will be good for you. You will begin to discover things about yourself you never knew were inside of you. The Lord will begin to show you the gifts He placed in you and you will be amazed at how purposeful you are and will be.

I want you to live your best life. The life The Lord has planned for you. I pray you are willing to grasp hold of that life and let go of the mediocre one you believe is it. It's not it. There's more. Yes, you are enough, but God wants to give you more. Stop settling for God's permissive will and embrace His Divine will. Stop sitting on the sidelines as everyone's cheerleader and get in the game and play. Imagine a game where everyone is not only allowed on the team, but is allowed to play and to win. It's not a competition and it's not a race, but a game that is fun and fulfilling. The Lord wants you on His team.

Pray this with me,

Father God, I thank You for life, I thank You for purpose, and I thank You for choosing me. Lord God, come into my life and rule my life. I accept You, Jesus, as my Lord and savior. Holy Spirit, I desire You as well. I desire that You will lead me every single day from this day forward. My life will never be the same and I am fully acceptant of the life that You have ahead of me. I will live, I will not die. I will not live a mediocre life and settle for Your permissive will, but I will be obedient and embrace Your divine will over my life. I will be whole and be healed so that I may help others

be whole and be healed. I will fulfill my dreams and I
believe that You will do all that You say You will do. Thank
You, Lord, for being so faithful. I cannot be perfect but I
can mature, help me continue to mature. Help me take what
I've learned and apply it in my life and the lives of those I
love. I love You Jesus. Thank You for loving me. In Jesus
Name, Amen.

*I will not die; instead, I will live
to tell what The Lord has done.*

Psalm 118:17 NLT

About the Author

Olivia Kristin Smith was born in Columbus, Ohio in the year 1992 by her biological parents Kim L. Leatherbury-Smith and Booker T. Smith. Olivia Smith is also the daughter of Morris Smith, whom her mother married and Bonitta Smith, who her father married. Olivia is the youngest of seven siblings and has always had a creative mind and been wise beyond her years. She moved to Pickerington, Ohio in the first grade where she continued in that school system until she graduated high school in 2010. As a child, Olivia always had a passion for dancing and the creative arts. She studied ballet, tap, jazz, and drama under the direction of China White at Theatre Street Dance Academy and was on an all-star hip-hop dance team. After high school, Olivia attended The University of Cincinnati and took after her mother to pursue her Bachelors of Science in Nursing degree. Olivia was extremely involved and ambitious on her college campus and she was always looking for the next great thing to become involved in. She was a mentor at the African American and Cultural Resource Center. She founded the organization AMBITION on the college of nursing campus for minority nursing students. She was a member of Alpha

204

Kappa Alpha Sorority Incorporated and was also inducted into two women's honorariums, Sigma Phi and The Lambda Society. After graduation, she moved back home to Columbus, Ohio and began to work as a registered nurse at Grant Medical Center.

Not long after returning home and beginning to work, Olivia realized that she wasn't as passionate about nursing as she thought she would be. After working at Grant hospital for one year she decided to transition to Nationwide Children's hospital so she could work with a younger population. During this time, Olivia bought a camera and realized she had a passion for photography. Only after 6 months of having her camera, people began to take interest in her work and she started a photography business called Olivia Kristin Photography the summer of 2016. Olivia had no idea that this photography business would be how The Lord was going to bring her back to Him. While being in an extremely toxic relationship, Olivia was hired by City of David to capture photos of their church service. At this service she received prayer and within two weeks she was out of the relationship. Olivia returned home to Christ at the beginning of 2017 and her life has not been the same. Olivia realized that everything she believed made her who she was, which was only blocking her from being who God called her to be in the first place. Olivia made the obedient decision to remove herself from the Greek organization, Alpha Kappa Alpha sorority incorporated, as well as making other lifestyle changes that were keeping her from being close to God. As the Lord began to mature Olivia into the woman of God she is today, He began to renew old desires and give her new desires that all relate to her purpose. Olivia began to write again, she began to read again, and she founded Can We Live, which is an online retail boutique that was launched as she wrote her first book, I Didn't Know I Was Dead.

Olivia is quite the entrepreneur and enjoys using her creativity to love and serve people. She manages Olivia Kristin Photography, Your Wedding Creatives with her older brother Jonathan, and Can We Live. She continues to work as a registered nurse part-time and teaches tap dance at For the Love of Dance School under the direction of Paris Miles. Olivia is a member and serves in the Personal Workers Ministry and God's Glory Dance Ministry at Rhema Christian Center under the leadership of Bishop LaFayette Scales. As a young single woman, Olivia has opportunities to travel many places and meet and network with diverse groups of people. Olivia is the youngest of seven siblings including from oldest to youngest: Latasha Winbush,

Latonia Byard, Noni Campbell, Michael Leatherbury, Marissa Iles, and Jonathan Smith. She loves Jesus, spending time with her family and friends, traveling, dancing, taking photos, and simply living life. Olivia believes her purpose in life is to share truth in a creative and non-conforming way. Whether that's through her writing, photography, clothing store, or simply being present, she wants to live, intentionally.

Explore what God is doing through Olivia...

BLOG
www.oliviakristin.com
Instagram/Facebook— @0liviakristin
E-mail— livtowrite@gmail.com

PHOTOGRAPHY
www.oliviakristinphotography.com
Instagram/Facebook— @oliviakristinphotography
E-mail— oliviakristinphotography@gmail.com

www.yourweddingcreatives.com
Instagram/Facebook— @yourweddingcreatives
E-mail— yourweddingcreatives@gmail.com

CAN WE *live*

CLOTHING STORE
www.canwelive.co
Instagram/Facebook— @shopcanwelive
E-mail— shopcanwelive@gmail.com

CONTACT
www.oliviakristin.com
IG/Facebook: @0liviakristin
livtowrite@gmail.com

Made in the USA
Columbia, SC
11 May 2019